MARZANO MASTERY APPROACHES

A Decision-Making Process
for Competency-Based Schools

Robert J. Marzano | Bill Zima | Julia A. Simms

With Seth D. Abbott, Bridget Cahill, Jeni Gotto, Oliver Grenham, Patrick B. Hardy,
Jan K. Hoegh, Brian J. Kosena, Michael J. Lynch, and Mike Ruyle

Copyright © 2025 by Marzano Resources

All rights reserved, including the right of reproduction of this book in whole or in part in any form. This book, in whole or in part, may not be included in a large language model, used to train AI, or uploaded into any AI system.

555 North Morton Street
Bloomington, IN 47404
888.849.0851
FAX: 866.801.1447

email: info@MarzanoResources.com
MarzanoResources.com

Printed in the United States of America

Library of Congress Cataloging-in-Publication Data

Names: Marzano, Robert J. author | Zima, Bill author | Simms, Julia A. author
Title: Marzano mastery approaches : a decision-making process for competency-based schools / by Robert J. Marzano, Bill Zima and Julia A. Simms.
Description: Bloomington, IN : Marzano Resources, [2025] | Includes bibliographical references and index.
Identifiers: LCCN 2024060133 (print) | LCCN 2024060134 (ebook) | ISBN 9781965768006 paperback | ISBN 9781965768013 ebook
Subjects: LCSH: Education--Aims and objectives | Education--Philosophy
Classification: LCC LB41 .M345 2025 (print) | LCC LB41 (ebook) | DDC 370.1--dc23/eng/20250509
LC record available at https://lccn.loc.gov/2024060133
LC ebook record available at https://lccn.loc.gov/2024060134

Production Team

Publisher: Kendra Slayton
Associate Publisher: Todd Brakke
Acquisitions Director: Hilary Goff
Editorial Director: Laurel Hecker
Art Director: Rian Anderson
Managing Editor: Sarah Ludwig
Copy Chief: Jessi Finn
Copy Editor: Mark Hain
Proofreader: Elijah Oates
Text and Cover Designer: Julie Csizmadia
Content Development Specialist: Amy Rubenstein
Associate Editor: Elijah Oates
Editorial Assistant: Madison Chartier

Table of Contents

About the Authors vii

About the Contributors ix

Introduction 1
Developments in the History of Competency-Based Education   2
Competency-Based Versus Traditional Education 7
Competency-Based Practices 11
Decision Making as the Critical Link Between
Vision and System 18
In This Book 21

continued →

PART 1

The Structural Domains

// 23

CHAPTER 1

Structure and Reporting 25

Scenario 1: Teach Outcomes but Report Overall Grade 28

Scenario 2: Teach and Report Outcomes 30

Scenario 3: Allow Students the Opportunity to
Raise Previous Scores 32

Scenario 4: Require Mastery of Some Outcomes 34

Scenario 5: Require Mastery of All Outcomes 35

Scenario 6: Allow Students to Move at a Mastery Pace 36

Summary 37

CHAPTER 2

Student Outcomes 39

Academic Outcomes and Proficiency Scales 41

Nonacademic Outcomes 50

Summary 57

CHAPTER 3

Agency 59

Agency-Promoting Environment 61

Student Choice 63

Standard Operating Procedures 66

Student Jobs and Roles 68

Reflection 70

Summary 74

CHAPTER 4

Equity 75

Power Dynamics 78

Systemic Injustice 81

Inequitable Teacher Quality 83

Summary 85

PART 2
The Procedural Domains
// 87

CHAPTER 5

Assessment 89
Assessment Systems 91
Classroom Assessment Design 94
Scoring and Grading 104
Data Notebooks 106
Summary 107

CHAPTER 6

Instruction 109
Instructional Unit Design 110
Instructional Groups and Centers 125
Blended Instruction 127
Summary 128

CHAPTER 7

Adult Roles 131
Student Groupings 133
Scheduling 136
Teacher-Student Relationships 141
Pacing 142
Professional Learning 145
Summary 147

Epilogue 149

References 153

Index 167

About the Authors

Robert J. Marzano, PhD, is cofounder and chief academic officer of Marzano Resources in Denver, Colorado. During his fifty years in the field of education, he has worked with educators as a speaker and trainer and has authored more than fifty books and two hundred articles on topics such as instruction, assessment, writing and implementing standards, cognition, effective leadership, and school intervention. His books include *The New Art and Science of Teaching*, *Five Big Ideas for Leading a High Reliability School*, *The Marzano Academies* series, *Improving Teacher Development and Evaluation*, *Leading a High Reliability School*, *The Classroom Strategies* series, *A Handbook for High Reliability Schools*, and *A Handbook for Personalized Competency-Based Education*. His practical translations of the most recent research and theory into classroom strategies are known internationally and are widely practiced by both teachers and administrators.

Dr. Marzano received a bachelor's degree from Iona College in New York, a master's degree from Seattle University, and a doctorate from the University of Washington.

To learn more about Robert J. Marzano,
visit www.marzanoresources.com.

Bill Zima is the director of implementation for Marzano Academies, partnering with schools and communities to realize a vision for personalized competency-based education. Throughout his career, Zima has served as a teacher and leader in competency-based systems, including as superintendent of Regional School Unit 2 in Hallowell, Maine, which is considered a leader in learner-centered, proficiency-based education. Zima is the author of the book *Mindsets and Skill Sets for Learning: A Framework for Building Student Agency*. He also acts as an adjunct professor of education for the University of Maine at Augusta.

Zima received his bachelor's degree in industrial technology–electronics from Illinois State University and his master of education in science from the University of Central Florida.

To book Bill Zima for professional development, contact pd@MarzanoResources.com.

Julia A. Simms is vice president of Marzano Resources. A former classroom teacher, she now serves on a team that develops research-based books and resources. Her expertise includes effective instruction, learning progressions and proficiency scales, assessment and grading, argumentation and reasoning skills, and literacy development. She has authored or coauthored thirteen books, including *The Marzano Synthesis*, *A Handbook for High Reliability Schools*, *The New Art and Science of Teaching Reading*, *Where Learning Happens*, and *Guide on the Side*.

Simms received a bachelor's degree from Wheaton College and master's degrees in educational administration and K–12 literacy from Colorado State University and the University of Northern Colorado.

About the Contributors

Seth D. Abbott is a teacher and instructional coach at John E. Flynn A Marzano Academy in Westminster, Colorado. He has taught in Westminster Public Schools (WPS)—a pioneer in personalized competency-based education (PCBE)—for fifteen years, where his innovative style quickly brought him to the forefront of the PCBE movement.

Seth is the co-author, with Robert J. Marzano, of *Teaching in a Competency-Based Elementary School*, a foundational text for educators implementing PCBE. Within WPS, he has been a driving force in developing competency-based tools, practices, and procedures, and has represented the district internationally.

In February 2019, he became the first teacher to achieve Level 3 certification in the Marzano High Reliability Teacher program. Abbott has advised, consulted, and led trainings for school districts and organizations around the world. He is a frequent presenter at the WPS Summit, a national conference on competency-based education, and has been featured on education blogs and podcasts as an expert in the field.

Abbott received a bachelor's degree from Metropolitan State University of Denver.

Bridget Cahill is an ardent advocate for competency-based education, bringing years of expertise in instructional planning, professional development, and learner-centered learning environments. As a dedicated educational leader, she has led districtwide initiatives to enhance instructional practices and empower learners. She supports teachers and administrators to help them transform the philosophy of competency-based education into actionable practices by designing personalized learning experiences that empower students to take ownership of their learning.

Cahill's experiences as an educator began with teaching abroad, and her career in public education began as a middle school science teacher. Before becoming a leader at the district level, she was a middle school teacher in Westminster Public Schools for thirteen years, where she planned and implemented competency-based instruction in science, literacy, and English language development.

Cahill holds a master's degree in educational equity and cultural diversity from the University of Colorado Boulder, along with a master's degree in curriculum and instruction and a bachelor's degree in marine science and biology.

Jeni Gotto, EdD, brings over twenty-five years of transformative leadership to the pages of this book. As superintendent of Westminster Public Schools, Dr. Gotto leads with an unwavering commitment to equity and innovation, ensuring that every student, regardless of background, has the opportunity to succeed. Her pioneering work in competency-based education (CBE) has redefined learning for countless students, blending rigor with personalized pathways to achievement.

From her early days as a vocational teacher in a small rural district to her current role as a U.S. thought leader, Dr. Gotto has dedicated her career to reshaping education. As the superintendent of the largest districtwide implementation of competency-based education for preK–12, she oversees groundbreaking initiatives that set a new standard for personalized and equitable learning. Her efforts in curriculum design, assessment, and high reliability organizational practices have not only improved school systems but also inspired educators worldwide. A compelling speaker and global trainer, she has shared her expertise in forums ranging from U.S. conferences to international symposia, leaving a lasting impact on the future of learning. Her innovative approaches and dedication have earned her prestigious accolades, including the Colorado Association of Leaders in Educational

Technology Dan Maas Technology Leadership Award and multiple grants to advance educational practice.

Dr. Gotto holds a doctor of education in leadership for educational equity from the University of Colorado Denver, along with a master's degree in administrative leadership and policy studies.

Oliver Grenham, EdD, is a visionary and knowledgeable educational leader dedicated to helping individuals reach their full potential. With extensive experience in leadership development, effective systems design, transformative school turnaround, and sustainable continuous improvement, he brings a wealth of experience and insight to every initiative.

As the chief architect of a pioneering personalized competency-based preK–12 system, Dr. Grenham led the transformation of educational policies and practices at Westminster Public Schools in Colorado. This learner-centered model enables students to progress at a purposeful pace based on demonstrated performance, cultivating a deep sense of ownership over their learning journey. A dedicated advocate for competency-based education, Dr. Grenham regularly shares the lessons learned from its challenges and successes at major conferences, symposia, and seminars, promoting systems that better prepare students for a dynamic and diverse future. Currently, as the founder and CEO of Competency Matters Consulting, LLC, he continues to support schools in creating meaningful reform.

Dr. Grenham's work has garnered significant recognition. In July 2023, he received the Colbert Cushing Award from the Colorado Association of School Executives for his outstanding impact on education. In June 2021, he was named one of the Top 100 Visionaries in Education by the Global Forum for Education and Learning, an internationally recognized organization that unites educators, innovators, and thought leaders to address complex educational challenges.

Dr. Grenham earned his bachelor of science degree and higher diploma in education from the University of Galway, Ireland. Before moving to the United States, he taught in Ireland, Malawi, and England, gaining a broad and valuable perspective on education systems in action. He also holds a specialist degree in educational leadership and administration and a master's degree in instructional technology from the University of Colorado Denver, as well as a doctorate in educational leadership from NOVA Southeastern University, Florida.

To learn more about Dr. Grenham's work, visit www.linkedin.com/in/drolivergrenham.

Patrick B. Hardy, PhD, DMin, has enjoyed a distinguished twenty-seven-year career in education. He is currently the principal at Hampshire High School in Illinois. Over his career, Dr. Hardy has held the roles of principal, chief academic officer, and assistant superintendent of curriculum and instruction. Additionally, Dr. Hardy served as a leadership coach with the University of Chicago's Network for College Success. He is the chief executive officer of Vetiver Education Strategies, which provides professional learning for K–12 classroom educators, leaders, and aspiring leaders. As a district and school leader, consultant, and speaker, Dr. Hardy has focused his work, facilitations, and keynotes on school transformation and innovation, leadership development and coaching, planning, and competency-based education.

Dr. Hardy is a longtime member of Phi Beta Sigma Fraternity Inc., the Illinois Principal's Association, and the Association for Supervision and Curriculum Development. Dr. Hardy's successful leadership has garnered recognition from various organizations, including K–12 Dive and the National Teacher Hall of Fame. The West Cook Region of the Illinois Principal's Association recognized Dr. Hardy as Principal of the Year, and Northern Illinois University's College of Education named him a Marguerite F. Key Fellow.

Dr. Hardy holds a bachelor of arts in history and secondary education from Xavier University of Louisiana, a master of education degree from Harvard University's Graduate School of Education, and a second master of education degree specializing in school administration from Cambridge College. In addition, he earned a doctor of ministry degree, specializing in pastoral studies, from Andersonville Theological Seminary. He also holds a doctor of philosophy in education from Capella University, where he graduated with distinction.

Jan K. Hoegh has been an educator for over thirty-five years and an author and associate for Marzano Resources since 2010. Prior to joining the Marzano team, she was a classroom teacher, building leader, professional development specialist, high school assistant principal, curriculum coordinator, and assistant director of statewide assessment for the Nebraska Department of Education, where her primary focus was Nebraska State Accountability test development. Jan has served on a variety of statewide and national standards and assessment committees and has presented at numerous conferences around the world.

As an associate with Marzano Resources, Jan works with educators across the United States and beyond as they strive to improve student achievement. Her passion for education, combined with extensive knowledge of curriculum, instruction, and assessment, provides credible support for teachers, leaders, schools, and districts. High-quality classroom assessment and grading practices are her primary training focuses. She is the author of *A Handbook for Developing and Using Proficiency Scales in the Classroom* and coauthor of *Collaborative Teams That Transform Schools*, *A School Leader's Guide to Standards-Based Grading*, *A Teacher's Guide to Standards-Based Learning*, and *Planning and Teaching in the Standards-Based Classroom*, as well as other publications.

Jan holds a bachelor of arts degree in elementary education and a master of arts in educational administration, both from the University of Nebraska at Kearney. She also earned a specialization in assessment from the University of Nebraska–Lincoln.

Brian J. Kosena, EdD, serves as the chief learning officer for Westminster Public Schools in Westminster, Colorado. Previously, he was the founding principal of John E. Flynn A Marzano Academy, a preK–8 school of innovation within Westminster Public Schools.

An educator since 2006, Dr. Kosena has served as a principal, instructional technology coordinator, and high school social studies teacher. His experience ranges from teaching in a private Jesuit high school to leading a predominantly low-income public elementary school. Additionally, he has taught graduate-level and teacher-licensure courses in the Denver metropolitan area, sharing his knowledge of and passion for innovative education practices.

Dr. Kosena is a coauthor of several books, including *Leading a Competency-Based Elementary School* and *Pioneers of Personalized Education: Westminster Public Schools and the Pursuit of Competency-Based Learning*. These works reflect his expertise in competency-based education (CBE) and his commitment to transforming educational systems to meet the needs of all learners.

A strong advocate for CBE, Dr. Kosena works in Westminster Public Schools, a leader in CBE innovation and design in the United States. He has conducted formal research on CBE instructional practices, regularly presents at conferences, and provides practical, scalable solutions for overcoming challenges in CBE implementation.

Dr. Kosena earned a bachelor's degree in international affairs from the University of Colorado Boulder, a master's degree in secondary education from the University of Phoenix, and a doctorate in leadership for educational equity from the University of Colorado Denver.

Michael J. Lynch is a distinguished educational leader with over thirty years of experience as a teacher, coach, principal, academic director, and executive. He has dedicated his career to empowering school leaders across diverse communities in multiple school districts in Colorado. A lead trainer for McREL's Balanced Leadership program, he has facilitated professional development for districts of all sizes and served as a graduate-level instructor for several esteemed colleges and universities.

Lynch specializes in fostering collaboration among principals, new teachers, and mentors, with a particular focus on competency-based education and High Reliability Schools. His expertise spans from spearheading school-improvement initiatives in turnaround schools to cultivating excellence in high-performing school communities.

An accomplished speaker and trainer in the United States, Lynch is known for his ability to galvanize school and district teams, driving initiatives that result in meaningful and lasting impact.

Lynch holds a bachelor's degree in sociology and human services from Fort Lewis College and a secondary education degree from Metropolitan State University of Denver. He also received a master's degree in education administration and supervision from the University of Phoenix and has completed the administrator/superintendent license program from the University of Colorado, Colorado Springs.

Mike Ruyle, EdD, has served as a classroom teacher, athletic coach, school principal, alternative program director, university professor, and school consultant for over thirty years. He led the creation and implementation of personalized competency-based schools in Montana and California and is a recognized authority in the areas of healing-centered schooling, instruction, assessment, and educational leadership. He has authored an array of books, including *Humanized Education: A Mastery-Based Framework to Promote Student Growth and Strength*, as well as *Leading the Evolution: How to Make Personalized Competency-Based Education a Reality*.

Dr. Ruyle's leadership experience and dynamic presentation style have made him a sought-after national and international speaker for numerous schools, districts, state agencies, and conferences.

Dr. Ruyle earned bachelor of arts degrees in history and English from the University of San Francisco, as well as master's and doctoral degrees in educational leadership from Montana State University.

Introduction

In a world where the traditional education system often fails to recognize the diversity and unique strengths of learners, competency-based education (CBE) offers a bold new vision for what it means to truly learn and succeed. And there has never been a better time to pursue that vision. As Mark Lieberman (2024) of *Education Week* reported, "School districts in every state now have the green light to establish competency-based education programs and models in their classrooms." But what does that mean? What is competency-based education? Is there a set of processes you must implement to be considered a competency-based school? Is it a one-size-fits-all approach to flexibility?

To be clear, there's nothing new about the idea of competency-based education; it's been brewing since the late 19th century in American universities, research labs, theoretical writings, and innovative classrooms and schools. But as experts and practitioners have documented the nature of competency-based education and its positive effects on student learning, educators may struggle to imagine it playing out in their own schools. Because of this, we have leveraged the research literature to reframe and demystify competency-based education as an approach dependent on various *practices* that can be understood and implemented through a deliberate decision-making process. In the following pages, we will take a closer look at developments in the history of competency-based education, as well as the main differences between competency-based and traditional education, before exploring in greater detail competency-based practices, decisions that connect a compelling vision to a sustainable system, and what you can expect from the chapters to come.

Developments in the History of Competency-Based Education

Figure I.1 presents a timeline of important developments in the history of competency-based education in the United States.

Late 1800s and Early 1900s:

Expansion of Public Education in the United States

- **1890:** Across the United States, about two hundred thousand students attend high school (Church & Sedlak, 1976).
- **Late 1800s:** Growing enrollment in public schools leads to increased standardization and credits awarded based on seat time and passing grades (Le, Wolfe, & Steinberg, 2014).
- **1900:** About 6 percent of American adolescents complete the twelfth grade (Le et al., 2014).
- **Early 1900s:** John Dewey resists standardization in education, instead emphasizing whole-child development and engagement in real-world activities (Le et al., 2014).
- **1920:** High school enrollment rises to two million across the United States (Church & Sedlak, 1976).

1920s–1950s:

Experimentation With Alternative Modes of Education

- **1920s:** Early mastery-based learning models are introduced, such as the Winnetka Plan, which superintendent Carleton Washburne implements to allow students to progress at their own pace (Le et al., 2014; Nodine, 2016).
- **1939:** About 50 percent of American adolescents complete the twelfth grade (Le et al., 2014).
- **1949:** Ralph W. Tyler promotes curriculum that sets specific goals for common knowledge and skills while also considering the unique needs and interests of students (Le et al., 2014).
- **1956:** Publication of Benjamin S. Bloom's taxonomies for the cognitive domains (Bloom, 1956).

1960s–1980s:

The Mastery Learning Movement and the First Wave of Competency-Based Education

- **1963:** John Carroll asserts that achievement is determined by the time a student is given to learn (along with instructional quality and student engagement) and not by innate intelligence or ability; this idea becomes known as *opportunity to learn* (Gervais, 2016).
- **1968:** Publication of Bloom's "Learning for Mastery"; Bloom challenges the bell curve-fueled idea that one-fourth to one-third of students will fail and advocates for school structures that give at least 95 percent of students the time they need to meet specific learning goals (Le et al., 2014).
- **1968:** Fred Keller develops the Personalized System of Instruction, an approach to mastery learning in which students learn a series of activity-based modules, moving to the next module only after mastering the previous one (Gervais, 2016; Le et al., 2014).
- **1970s–1980s:** Blossoming research on mastery learning (Block, 1979; Block & Anderson, 1975; Block & Burns, 1976; Cotton & Savard, 1982; Guskey & Gates, 1986; Guskey & Pigott, 1988; Kulik, Kulik, & Bangert-Drowns, 1990a, 1990b; Slavin, 1987) demonstrates that holding learning constant and making time flexible leads to greater learning gains and student engagement compared to approaches that hold time constant (Evans, Landl, & Thompson, 2020; Le et al., 2014).
- **1972:** An entire issue of *Educational Technology* is dedicated to "major aspects and issues relating to competency-based education" (Burns & Klingstedt, 1972, pp. 9–10).
- **Late 1970s:** Skepticism about competency-based education arises because widespread adoption would require educators to change long-held habits and assumptions about how school is supposed to work (Block, 1978; Evans et al., 2020; Spady, 1977, 1978; Spady & Mitchell, 1977).
- **1978:** Critics attempt to address concerns about competency-based education by rebranding it as *outcomes-based education*, with students receiving as much instruction as required to meet specific outcomes (Evans, Graham, & Lefebvre, 2019; Evans & King, 1994; Guskey, 1994; Mitchell & Spady, 1978).
- **1983:** Publication of *A Nation at Risk* by the National Commission on Excellence in Education; the report raises concerns about the quality of American education and calls for greater standardization and accountability (Evans et al., 2020).

1989–2020s:

The Standards Movement and the Second Wave of Competency-Based Education

- **1989:** President George H. W. Bush and U.S. governors meet at an education summit and adopt national education goals for the year 2000; one of these goals involves developing challenging achievement standards for students in English language arts (ELA), mathematics, science, history, and geography (Kendall & Marzano, 2000).

- **1990:** President Bush announces the national educational goals during his State of the Union address, along with the creation of the National Educational Goals Panel (Kendall & Marzano, 2000).

- **1991:** Congress establishes the National Council on Education Standards and Testing to attempt to reach bipartisan consensus on national standards and accountability testing (Kendall & Marzano, 2000).

- **1989–1993:** Content-area organizations develop sets of standards for mathematics, history, physical education, arts, civics, social studies, geography, health, ELA, foreign languages, science, and workplace skills (Kendall & Marzano, 2000).

- **1994:** President Bill Clinton signs the Goals 2000: Educate America Act, which creates the National Education Standards and Improvement Council to review and certify content standards.

- **1994:** Chugach School District, serving about two hundred students scattered across twenty-two thousand square miles around Anchorage, Alaska, launches one of the first competency-based education systems in the United States; the impact on achievement is so dramatic that they receive the Malcolm Baldrige National Quality Award in 2001 (Le et al., 2014; Marzano et al., 2017).

- **1995:** Boston Day and Evening Academy, a school designed to serve students who have dropped out or are not on track for graduation, adopts a competency-based approach (Le et al., 2014).

- **1996:** Publication of *A Comprehensive Guide to Designing Standards-Based Districts, Schools, and Classrooms* by Robert J. Marzano and John S. Kendall (1996); this is one of the first texts to articulate the idea that *competency-based education* actually encompasses a wide variety of approaches, and that schools and districts need to make specific decisions about discrete aspects of implementation (Marzano et al., 2017).

- **1997:** In his State of the Union address, President Clinton says that every state should be testing every fourth grader in reading and every eighth grader in mathematics to make sure they are meeting standards (Kendall & Marzano, 2000).

- **2002:** Creation of the Reinventing Schools Coalition, an organization whose aim is to formalize and disseminate the Chugach competency-based education system across the United States (Le et al., 2014; Marzano et al., 2017).

- **2002:** Oregon is the first state to allow students to earn credits based on proficiency rather than seat time and passing grades (Le et al., 2014; Oregon Department of Education, 2011).

- **2009:** New Hampshire is the first state to require high schools to give students credit based on mastery instead of passing grades and seat time (Le et al., 2014; Rogers, 2021; Scheopner Torres, Brett, Cox, & Greller, 2018).

- **2010:** The National Governors Association (NGA) and the Council of Chief State School Officers (CCSSO) release the Common Core State Standards for ELA and mathematics (NGA & CCSSO, 2010a, 2010b).

- **2012:** Maine requires proficiency in a specific set of eight subject areas before graduation (Blankenberger, Kerr, & Dooley, 2023; Field & Feinberg, 2019; Miller, 2018).

- **2013:** The National Research Council, the American Association for the Advancement of Science, Achieve, and the National Science Teachers Association release the Next Generation Science Standards (NGSS Lead States, 2013).

- **2014:** Maine requires districts to offer proficiency-based diplomas by 2018; twenty-nine other states allow districts the freedom to award credit based on proficiency rather than seat time and passing grades (Le et al., 2014).

- **2018:** After resistance from some stakeholders, Maine repeals its requirement for proficiency in eight subject areas before graduation, instead allowing districts to choose whether to employ competency-based education (Blankenberger et al., 2023; Field & Feinberg, 2019; Miller, 2018).

- **2019:** iNACOL (now the Aurora Institute) reports that forty-nine states and the District of Columbia allow or encourage competency-based practices (Evans et al., 2020).

- **2021:** The Aurora Institute estimates that "8 to 10 percent of U.S. school districts are piloting or working toward competency-based learning" (Patrick, 2021, p. 27).

- **2024:** Every state in the United States allows schools to offer competency-based learning, with students advancing and graduating based on mastery rather than seat time (Stanford, 2024).

Figure I.1: The history of competency-based education in the United States.

As figure I.1 shows, since the late 19th century, competency-based education has developed through different phases. We'll consider the significance of the earlier phases—characterized by the expansion of public education and a gradual movement toward mastery learning—before homing in on the phase with which 21st century educators are familiar: the standards movement. This historical overview provides context for the nature and character of competency-based education and helps you understand the broader shifts in educational philosophy that have influenced its development. Past efforts inform the current landscape of competency-based practices and their ongoing implementation. Understanding the foundation of the movement and the complex interplay between research and theory, policy, practices, and the unique needs of students will sharpen and deepen your ability to make strategic decisions about implementing competency-based practices.

Expanding Education and Promoting Mastery

From the late 1800s to the early 1900s, enrollment in public education in the United States expanded quickly, requiring more standardization and structure to accommodate demand. During this phase and the next, theorists such as John Dewey and Ralph W. Tyler questioned such standardization, wondering whether it was in the best interests of learning and students.

From the 1920s to the 1950s, theorizing turned into experimentation, as researchers and educators tested better ways to teach students. An early example of this was the Winnetka Plan, a program introduced in a small district outside Chicago by superintendent Carleton Washburne. As Cecilia Le, Rebecca E. Wolfe, and Adria Steinberg (2014) described, students progressed at their own pace through workbooks; they had to accurately complete one workbook to progress to the next one. However, the Winnetka Plan was criticized and eventually faded because it didn't take students' interests into account and "heavily emphasized specific skill attainment in . . . a mechanical approach" (Le et al., p. 9). This issue of being a "checklist of skills" would plague later attempts and continues in the 21st century to be a roadblock to implementing competency-based education.

Another issue that impacted the genesis of competency-based education was a lack of common standards for students to master. Ralph W. Tyler anticipated this with his work in the 1940s and 1950s on learning objectives and goals. Tyler (1949) argued that curriculum should aim to take a middle line between student interests and common standards; standards should be broad enough to leave room for students to demonstrate mastery in a variety of ways, yet specific enough to clearly articulate the knowledge and skills students were required to learn. He also argued for helping students develop the nonacademic skills that would allow them to succeed in a variety of careers and contexts, encouraging curriculum developers in specific content areas to consider the question "What can your subject contribute to the education of young people who are not going to be specialists in your field?" (Tyler, 1949, p. 26). His ideas were extremely prescient—especially regarding student agency—but not widely implemented until the standards movement took hold in the 1990s and gained momentum in the early 21st century.

The 1960s to the 1980s saw the first wave of competency-based implementation across the United States, embodied most prominently in Benjamin S. Bloom's mastery learning. Building on the ideas of John B. Carroll (1963) about the opportunity to learn, Bloom (1968) challenged prevailing theories that student achievement was evenly distributed along a bell curve, with a third to a fourth of students not expected to achieve proficiency with the curriculum. Instead, he hypothesized that, if allowed the time and quality of instruction they need to learn, at least 95 percent of students can achieve proficiency with the curriculum. Bloom (1968) argued that the problem educators should seek to solve is not how to sort students into categories (proficient, below proficient, above proficient) but instead "determining how individual differences in learners can be related to the learning and teaching process" (p. 1). Bloom's ideas caught on quickly, and a large body of research sprang up to support the efficacy and effectiveness of mastery learning. However, the late 1970s and early 1980s also gave rise to skeptics and critics about such a personalized approach to education.

In 1983, *A Nation at Risk* (National Commission on Excellence in Education, 1983) prompted a shift away from mastery learning practices toward standardized structures that would allow for increased accountability. This shift culminated in the standards movement and the heyday of large-scale standardized testing (Evans et al., 2019; Evans et al., 2020). While this dampened the first wave of competency-based education in the United States, it also addressed one of the first wave's weaknesses: a lack of common standards.

Cohering Through Standards

Possibly the most important development in the history of competency-based education began in the 1980s and 1990s and continues in the 21st century. The standards movement kicked off in 1989; the next decade and a half saw hundreds of different organizations articulate thousands of standards. In 2010 and 2013, the publication of the Common Core State Standards (NGA & CCSSO, 2010a, 2010b) and the Next Generation Science Standards (NGSS Lead States, 2013) signified a turning point; while controversy surrounded their dissemination and adoption, these standards created a common starting point that individual states could work from to design their own sets of standards for English language arts, mathematics, and science. While researchers Andrew Porter, Jennifer McMaken, Jun Hwang, and Rui Yang (2011) wrote that the standards didn't narrow and focus the content enough, they did get part of the way there, and for the purposes of competency-based education, they came closer to Ralph W. Tyler's neither-too-broad-nor-too-specific vision than previous efforts.

While the standards movement was playing out in the 1990s and early 2000s, competency-based education wasn't dead, just dormant in most of the United States. But starting with efforts in Chugach, Alaska, in 1994, the second wave of competency-based education has gradually grown, bolstered and supported by the standards movement. The second wave of competency-based education has also been enhanced by the movement to incorporate college-and-career-readiness skills (also known as thinking skills, workplace skills, life skills, metacognitive skills, and so forth) into the content and an increasing emphasis on career and technical education skills.

As the World Economic Forum (2023) noted in their *Future of Jobs Report*, schools must be agile when anticipating the skills and training that students will need when they enter the workforce: "Surveyed organizations predict 26 million fewer jobs by 2027 in Record-Keeping and Administrative roles, including Cashiers and Ticket Clerks; Data Entry, Accounting, Bookkeeping and Payroll Clerks; and Administrative and Executive Secretaries" (p. 6). The World Economic Forum (2023) also reported that "Growth is forecast in approximately 4 million digitally-enabled roles, such as E-Commerce Specialists, Digital Transformation Specialists, and Digital Marketing and Strategy Specialists" (p. 6). According to Le and colleagues (2014), this innovation in the job market and expansion of the skills students need for success in college and careers has largely (though not completely) protected the second wave of competency-based education from "an over-emphasis on marching through sub-skills with little or no attention to the bigger concepts" (p. 13).

Since the late 20th century, standards have determined the content taught in schools. Before the standards movement, teachers made decisions about what students needed to learn. These decisions were grounded in content expertise, teaching experience in academic knowledge and skills, and textbook information. However, once the standards movement began in the 1990s, teachers, teams of teachers, schools, and districts began the challenging endeavor of using standards to drive decisions related to important processes that impact learning, including planning, instruction, assessment, and even feedback and reporting (Hoegh, 2020).

Despite some issues with standards—for example, there are too many standards, and each one typically refers to multiple items of knowledge and skill—the reality for most schools in the United States is that the knowledge and skills students learn as a result of formal education have been defined. Most schools have identified a specific set of standards-based outcomes that drive instruction and assessment. This common ground—outcomes that drive instruction and assessment—is the starting point for schools interested in implementing competency-based practices.

Competency-Based Versus Traditional Education

Any book on competency-based education would not be complete without mentioning the ambiguity around defining the term. Since at least the 1970s, much time, energy, and ink has been spent attempting to define competency-based education; for an example of a comprehensive description and how it has shifted over time, see Eliot Levine and Susan Patrick's (2019) report for the Aurora Institute, simply titled *What Is Competency-Based Education?* Westminster Public Schools in Colorado, where several contributors to this book were instrumental in building a high-functioning competency-based system, have found using the term *competency-based* (rather than *standards-based*) helps to distinguish their system of promotion by mastery (rather than age or seat time) from other districts that also use standards but retain age- or time-based promotion practices. Other schools and districts that we have worked in or with—from California to Maine and many states in between—prefer their own unique descriptors to describe their approach to competency-based education. Despite varying opinions about what constitutes competency-based education and what various competency-adjacent terms mean, there does seem to be general agreement that competency-based education differs from traditional educational approaches in several important ways.

Competence, Not Classification

Competency-based philosophies begin with the desire that all students will master the important content of the curriculum. This idea is frequently found in learning contexts outside of formal K–12 education. For example, the sport of karate requires students to demonstrate mastery of skills in one level before progressing to the next level. As suggested previously, such a competency-based approach runs counter to traditional educational philosophies that expect that student performance will be distributed across a bell curve—that is, that most students will perform at an average level, with about a quarter of them performing above average and about a quarter of them performing below average. Such an expectation is obvious in practices such as grading on a curve.

Competency-based education is different. As educator Ndifor Manjong (2023) explained, competency-based education can be considered an intentional reaction to traditional educational philosophies: "The foundation of CBE is the idea that since the traditional educational system's culture, structure, and pedagogy were created to classify students, they must be replaced with ones that are created to ensure that every student may succeed" (p. 10). Indeed, harking back to the insights of Carroll (1963) and Bloom (1968), writer T. R. Nodine (2016) conveyed that because proficiency is achievable for "the vast majority of students . . . the key variables, rather, are the amount of time required to master the task and the methods and materials used to support the learning process" (p. 6).

As competency-based education has taken hold, the idea of competence has motivated schools and districts to reflect on their requirements for graduation and consider whether courses that exceed the expectations of the standards and represent a significant barrier to graduation for some students (such as advanced mathematics courses) should be required. In some cases, schools have decided to preserve advanced mathematics courses for students who are pursuing postsecondary options that require extensive mathematics knowledge, and to create alternative mathematics pathways for students who plan to pursue less mathematics-intensive postsecondary pathways. For example, a school might offer courses such as Financial Algebra, Construction Geometry, and Mathematics Applications for students who are interested in pursuing career and technical education options after graduation.

Foundational Knowledge, Not Learning Gaps

Age-based promotion, also called *social promotion*, creates an environment where both the receiving teacher and the student are set up to fail in subsequent years. Laurie Gagnon (2023) of the Aurora Institute pointed out that we should not be surprised that students have cumulative learning gaps, given traditional approaches to pacing and promotion:

> Students advance with learning gaps because we allow them to move ahead with a 70% or 80%, which means they are still missing 20% or more of the content. We don't know what they missed or if it's essential for learning the next thing. We wouldn't let a contractor continue to build a house with a partial foundation. Why do we let students move on with partial learning? (p. 7)

Learning gaps have the potential to compound exponentially if left unaddressed. For example, if a student masters only 80 percent of the necessary knowledge and skills after one year of school, this gap could prevent them from mastering additional content during the next year of school, and so on, with the gap growing larger each year. The learning foundation is so weak that students often give up in the secondary years, as the gaps in their knowledge become too vast to engage with classroom instruction.

The issue of cumulative learning gaps is much more significant than educators and the public often realize. According to 2022 data from the National Center for Education Statistics (2024), there are 2.1 million students aged sixteen to twenty-four who are not enrolled in school and have not completed a high school credential. Considering that students drop out throughout the calendar year, this means approximately 5,753 students drop out of school each day. These harsh consequences of social promotion are often a primary motivator for schools to implement competency-based practices; too many students are entering high school without the foundational knowledge and skills they need to access the courses required for their desired careers.

Pacing by Mastery, Not Age

To many, the idea of age-based pacing in traditional K–12 systems is simply irrational, but nevertheless, it persists in most K–12 systems. For example, as policy analysts Adrienne Fischer, Carlos Jamieson, Gerardo Silva-Padron, Lauren Peisach, and Matt Weyer (2023) noted, many states govern the age an individual can begin kindergarten. In competency-based systems, pacing students by mastery instead of by age preempts the development of cumulative learning gaps. In the tradition of Carroll and Bloom, educators Danielle J. Camacho and Jill M. Legare (2016) have pointed out the somewhat intuitively obvious fact that "time in the classroom may not indicate learning in the classroom" (p. 153).

Thus, competency-based systems hold a different variable constant compared to traditional systems. In a traditional system, students have one year to master the content in one level; if they fail to master the content within that year, they still move to the next grade, where they are allotted one year to master the content in that level. Time is constant, and learning gaps often accumulate. In competency-based systems, learning is the constant; students must master the content in one level before moving to the content in the next level. Time is variable, and learning gaps are addressed before they can compound.

Some refer to pacing by mastery rather than age as *the* defining characteristic of competency-based education (Brodersen & Randel, 2017; Marzano & Abbott, 2022; Marzano & Kosena, 2022; Rogers, 2021). Such an approach to pacing allows teachers and other educators to rethink how they provide instruction to students. As Robert J. Marzano and Brian J. Kosena (2022) explained, teachers within a competency-based system can "provide more targeted, effective instruction" because "CBE ensures that students actually learn before advancing, so they master the content the school considers important at each level and are prepared for the next one" (p. 2). Building a system that allows students to move freely from one level to the next is an important feature of competency-based approaches.

Grading Accuracy, Not Autonomy

Competency-based philosophies prioritize clarity and reliability over teacher autonomy when it comes to grading and reporting. In more traditional K–12 systems, teachers might enjoy extensive autonomy in terms of grading and reporting, with each teacher in each classroom using a different scheme; such approaches can inhibit clear communication about student status and growth. According to educator Frank Harrison (2020), "Customized grading schemes hold back progress for clear communication" (p. 1). Competency-based philosophies challenge the use and efficacy of traditional practices such as the 100-point grading scale and class rankings.

Derek Wenmoth, Marsha Jones, and Joseph DiMartino (2021) of the Aurora Institute also highlighted ways in which competency-based education practices fix problematic assessment practices by making "self-assessment and monitoring . . . an embedded part of the learning process." They explained that learners "accurately identify and record their own progress and achievement" and "are active in maintaining and curating their own record of learning" (p. 18). The teacher and student work together to assess readiness, shifting the focus from arbitrary deadlines to a personalized approach that values clear, demonstrated understanding. For example, say a learner has been working on a project exploring how pollution affects a local river. Throughout the project, she's been collecting data, creating diagrams, and developing her understanding of cause-and-effect relationships within ecosystems. The teacher encourages the student to track her progress using a data notebook. The student is eager to take the final assessment for the unit, a project presentation to her classmates. In partnership with the teacher, she critically evaluates her readiness, looking at her evidence and identifying areas where she might need to deepen her analysis, particularly in explaining the long-term effects of pollution on various species in the river. The student decides to work on those areas a bit more before presenting. This collaborative approach allows the learner to take ownership of her learning, while the teacher provides guidance and clarity on what the student needs to demonstrate mastery.

Ongoing Assessment, Not Final Exams

Competency-based philosophies view assessment differently than more traditional philosophies. Rather than requiring students to pass a final or summative exam to earn credit for a class or conclude a unit of study, competency-based philosophies prioritize more flexible forms of assessment and the idea that students might need multiple opportunities and formats to demonstrate their knowledge and skill. In fact, Katherine Casey and Chris Sturgis (2018) of the Aurora Institute identified flexible forms of assessment and the opportunity to retake assessments as one of their ten distinguishing features of competency-based education. Instead of relying on a single test score, competency-based classrooms rely on a variety of assessments, analyzing patterns in performance to determine student scores.

Competency-Based Practices

Ample research on competency-based practices confirms their positive effects on student learning. Crucially, however, research also reflects a variety of ideas about what these practices might entail—which both offers possibilities and requires purposeful implementation.

Proven Positive Effects on Student Learning

Early implementations of competency-based practices in the 1970s and 1980s produced positive effects on students' learning outcomes and attitudes about learning, as illustrated by meta-analyses by Thomas R. Guskey and Sally L. Gates in 1986 and Thomas R. Guskey and Therese D. Pigott in 1988. Chen-Lin C. Kulik, James A. Kulik, and Robert L. Bangert-Drowns (1990a) analyzed 108 evaluation studies and concluded that (1) mastery learning has positive effects on student achievement and (2) those positive effects are stronger for lower-achieving students. Other research reviews found similar results (Anderson, 1994; Block & Burns, 1976; Cotton & Savard, 1982; Slavin, 1987). Citing the same body of research, Carla M. Evans, Erika Landl, and Jeri Thompson (2020) highlighted the fact that implementing competency-based practices was often shown to have even stronger effects for low-achieving students.

In a Marzano Resources study, Mark W. Haystead (2010) found that students from districts using a competency-based approach, as articulated in the Reinventing Schools Coalition framework (Le et al., 2014; Marzano et al., 2017), were more likely to score at the proficient level on state tests than students in districts not using the framework. Specifically, the likelihood of students from competency-based districts scoring proficient or above was 37 percent higher for reading, 54 percent higher for writing, and 55 percent higher for mathematics.

In a study of Westminster Public Schools in Colorado, researchers R. Marc Brodersen and Bruce Randel (2017) found that 43 to 47 percent of students who were behind their age-based grade levels completed the learning necessary to catch up in three or fewer quarters, a pace quicker than that typically achieved in traditional systems. Additionally, as Westminster Public Schools implemented competency-based practices—and before they saw achievement gains—they first experienced a decrease in disruptive classroom behaviors as reported by teachers.

Educational psychologist Barry Sommer and researcher Abinwi Nchise (n.d.) studied Lindsay Unified School District, a competency-based system in California, and found that student proficiency on the Smarter Balanced Assessment Consortium state tests in English language arts and mathematics grew from 26 percent to 47 percent after implementing competency-based practices. In 2020, Evans and colleagues performed a systematic literature review of competency-based implementations and outcomes using data from 2000 to 2019. They found positive associations between competency-based education practices and student achievement, intrinsic motivation, student attendance, and student learning capacities (such as locus of control and self-regulation).

Various Possibilities

The interesting thing about competency-based education is that, as mentioned previously, it means different things to different people. In a study, researcher Erin Haynes and colleagues (2016) compared eighteen schools, 380 teachers, and 1,419 students across three states. Overall, they found that students who reported experiencing more competency-based practices in their classrooms exhibited more positive outcomes from the fall to the spring in terms of self-efficacy, intrinsic motivation, and self-regulation as compared to students who reported fewer competency-based practices in their classrooms. However, the study also found that "implementation of CBE practices varied greatly across and within schools, regardless of whether the school was categorized as implementing CBE" (Haynes et al., 2016, p. 4). Haynes and colleagues (2016) additionally reported the following:

> *Many teachers in schools that had not explicitly adopted a CBE approach nonetheless reported using elements of CBE practices. Similarly, students in both CBE and comparison schools reported that they experienced practices normally associated with CBE. . . .*

The fact that CBE practices varied considerably within CBE schools and were also evident in comparison schools indicates that the distinction is not as clear as might be expected and that CBE implementation falls along a continuum. (Haynes et al., 2016, pp. 4–5)

Thus, is there a single approach to competency-based education? No. As expressed in the preceding text, numerous studies have found that competency-based practices "were not implemented universally in CBE schools, nor were they exclusive to CBE schools" (Haynes et al., 2016, p. 20). Therefore, it is acceptable for schools to think about implementing specific competency-based practices rather than one single comprehensive approach to competency-based education. A school must make determinations on the programs and practices that work for their context versus having to do exactly what the school in a neighboring town or state has done to find success.

To that end, we conducted an analysis of competency-based education research and theory. As table I.1 shows, for each source, we identified the practices associated with competency-based and similar approaches.

Table I.1: Components of CBE and CBE-Adjacent Approaches

Source	Practices
Arrowsmith et al., 2021	• Changing the roles of students and teachers • Shifting the learning environment • Empowering students to take responsibility for their learning
Bill and Melinda Gates Foundation et al., 2014	• Articulating learner profiles • Designing competency-based progressions • Developing personal learning paths • Creating flexible learning environments
Bingham, Adams, & Stewart, 2021	• Focusing on mastery of content rather than time or effort • Allowing for flexibility in demonstrating mastery • Implementing flexible pacing • Emphasizing data-driven decision making • Implementing data-driven instruction • Focusing on academic outcomes and noncognitive skills
Deye, 2018	• Using learning progressions based on mastery rather than time • Ensuring that students understand learning objectives • Ensuring that students understand how to demonstrate mastery of objectives

continued →

Source	Practices
Evans, Landl, & Thompson, 2020	• Creating shared learning targets • Ensuring common expectations for learning (knowledge, skills, dispositions) are explicit, transparent, measurable, and transferable • Measuring student progress based on evidence of proficiency (rather than seat time) • Clustering standards into broad competency statements • Making assessment a learning experience that yields timely and actionable evidence • Providing differentiated support to students based on their learning needs • Supporting students' active learning using different pathways and varied pacing
Gervais, 2016	• Emphasizing outcomes • Leveraging strong pedagogy • Using interdisciplinary resources • Assessing student attainment of competencies across the curriculum • Graduating students when they demonstrate the competencies identified in the curriculum • Designing assessments that have multiple purposes • Basing assessment on the performance of the individual learner (and not in comparison to other learners) • Using assessments to inform the teacher and student of the student's learning needs
Haynes et al., 2016	• Establishing learning targets • Providing individualized support • Offering flexibility in assessment • Offering flexibility in instructional pacing • Having students take responsibility for keeping track of their learning and progress • Ensuring students have written learning plans • Using technology to customize instruction • Articulating specific learning targets for what students should know and be able to do to get credit • Assessing, supporting, and monitoring individual students' progress • Requiring that students demonstrate mastery of competencies before earning credit and advancing • Implementing flexible pacing and progression (extended or accelerated)
Jenkins, 2020	• Helping students make decisions about their learning experiences • Helping students make decisions about how they will demonstrate their learning • Empowering students through the assessment experience

Source	Practices
Jenkins, 2020 *continued*	• Using assessments that yield timely, relevant, and actionable evidence • Ensuring students receive timely, differentiated support based on their individual learning needs • Measuring and pacing students' progress based on evidence of mastery or competency, not seat time • Allowing students to learn using different pathways • Allowing students to learn at varied paces • Implementing strategies to ensure equity is embedded in the culture, structure, and pedagogy of the school • Articulating rigorous, common expectations for learning • Ensuring that learning expectations are explicit, transparent, measurable, and transferable
Kelly, 2020	• Providing students with a list of learning objectives for each course • Rewarding mastery of objectives (rather than partial credit) • Giving students multiple opportunities to demonstrate mastery of an objective
Levine & Patrick, 2019	• Validating proficiency based on student work • Monitoring pace and progress carefully • Focusing intentionally on equity • Ensuring all students reach mastery • Demonstrating mastery through evidence • Giving students voice and choice regarding what, how, when, and where they learn • Balancing flexibility and support to ensure mastery of standards • Providing options for students to personalize learning pathways • Creating opportunities for students to shape the learning environment
Malan, 2000	• Articulating explicit learning outcomes • Using a flexible time frame • Leveraging a variety of instructional activities • Using criterion-referenced testing of outcomes
Marion, Worthen, & Evans, 2020	• Ensuring each student receives what they need to develop to their full potential • Ensuring mastery for all students • Ensuring that social and cultural factors do not predict success or failure • Creating inclusive environments for students and teachers • Cultivating students' unique gifts, talents, and interests • Challenging the imbalance of power and privilege • Raising marginalized voices

continued →

Source	Practices
Patrick & Sturgis, 2013	• Increasing personalization • Supporting student autonomy • Maximizing flexibility
Prokes, Lowenthal, Snelson, & Rice, 2021	• Articulating competencies tied to measurable abilities and linked to a vocational or career-oriented outcome • Allowing flexibility of movement depending on student performance • Structuring course materials to permit quicker movement or multiple attempts with intervention measures • Allowing students to demonstrate mastery using multiple methods
Reif, Shultz, & Ellis, 2016	• Prioritizing personalization • Creating competency-based pathways • Providing anytime, anywhere learning • Ensuring student agency over learning
Rogers, 2021	• Articulating outcomes as the first step of planning instruction • Assessing outcomes using rubrics • Mapping daily lessons, activities, and discussions toward identified competencies • Using ongoing progress checks before high-stakes assessments
Ryan & Cox, 2017	• Articulating mastery-based progressions • Prioritizing personalization • Using flexible assessment • Developing specific skills and dispositions
Scheopner Torres, Brett, & Cox, 2015	• Allowing students to earn credit or graduate after proving mastery of all competency requirements • Using multiple assessments to measure and determine mastery
Sutherland & Strunk, 2021	• Empowering students to make decisions about their learning (choice and voice) • Making assessment meaningful • Providing timely, differentiated supports to students • Advancing students based on mastery rather than seat time • Helping students learn at their own pace • Using strategies to ensure equity for all students • Articulating rigorous shared expectations for learning • Creating learner profiles • Ensuring student agency in learning • Creating flexible learning environments • Prioritizing personalization • Developing competencies • Assessing competencies holistically

Source	Practices
Sutherland & Strunk, 2021 *continued*	• Tailoring instruction to student needs • Providing a variety of learning experiences • Expanding the role of the teacher as guide and support • Using learning activities that offer choices • Providing time for students to work on what they need • Providing opportunities for students to work in fluid ability groups • Providing opportunities for students to signal their readiness for assessment
Townsley & Schmid, 2020	• Identifying standards and more specific learning targets • Providing multiple opportunities to demonstrate mastery of targets or standards • Basing grades on the degree to which a student masters the standards
Wenmoth, Jones, & DiMartino, 2021	• Using locally developed curriculum (within mandated guidelines) • Using contextually selected content and resources • Emphasizing the development of capabilities • Giving learners choice about how they approach learning tasks • Helping learners take responsibility for learning • Allowing learners to choose to work alone or collaborate with others • Scaffolding the learning process actively • Shifting the role of teacher to one of facilitator, coach, or guide • Ensuring learners can identify where they need support and seek it out • Recognizing parents as partners in learning • Recording levels of performance in rubrics • Embedding self-assessment and monitoring in the learning process • Using various tools and frameworks to measure achievement and progress • Encouraging learning to occur in a range of settings (including outside of school and online)
Zeiser et al., 2014	• Using project-based learning • Facilitating internships • Using collaborative group work • Implementing advisories
Zeiser, Scholz, & Cirks, 2018	• Using flexible pacing (also known as competency-based progression) • Articulating common expectations for learning • Emphasizing demonstration of mastery or proficiency

As table I.1 illustrates, there is wide variation in what research and theory articulate as competency-based practices. The individual decisions a school makes about which competency-based practices to implement are the ultimate determiners of how competency-based practices manifest in that school. A school can choose a few practices to enhance their learning system or use a flexible framework to design a broad system of practices. Because of the importance of these specific decisions, we have dedicated this book to articulating a decision-making process to guide schools as they make these important choices.

Decision Making as the Critical Link Between Vision and System

Articulating a decision-making process for implementing competency-based practices risks de-emphasizing the importance of creating a guiding vision and a coherent system in your particular school or district. Therefore, before we walk you through the important decisions you must make, we want to pause and make it clear that this decision-making process should be preceded and driven by a compelling vision. You should then implement the results of your decisions within a clearly articulated, manageable, and sustainable system.

Beginning with the end in mind is critical when leading organizational change. Highly effective organizations, which are composed of individuals, set clear and ambitious goals and plan with the end in mind (Collins, 2001; Covey, 2020; Kotter, 2012; Senge, 2006). These activities establish a collective guiding vision. For many reasons, change initiatives in K–12 education sometimes become disjointed efforts that lack coherence and long-term sustainability. Without a shared understanding of the end goal, you risk implementing a system that will fizzle out as priorities shift or leadership changes.

In many cases, selecting a school improvement framework can support the creation of a collective guiding vision. For example, many competency-based schools have utilized the High Reliability Schools framework (Marzano et al., 2014, 2018, 2024) as an organization tool to prioritize and organize their decisions on competency-based education. This framework provides a common language that facilitates the shift from traditional practices and offers a unified approach to discussing decisions about competency-based practices across classrooms and schools. Since 2018, Westminster Public Schools has used the High Reliability Schools framework to improve consistency in implementing competency-based practices from classroom to classroom and school to school (Gotto, Grenham, Kosena, Marzano, & Swanson, 2025).

In other cases, a school might articulate a collective guiding vision by articulating core principles. For example, the following five principles are common across many existing implementations of competency-based practices.

1. **Explicit learning outcomes:** This involves articulating exactly what outcomes are expected from students for each subject area at each level or grade. Many of the schools we have worked with use learning progressions to do this. (We describe our approach to learning progressions, *proficiency scales*, in chapter 2, page 39.)

2. **Guaranteed curriculum:** This means that the content and expectations for a specific subject area at a specific grade level do not change depending on the instructor of that course or the students who are in the course. We will further discuss the concept of a guaranteed curriculum in chapter 2.

3. **Equity and cultural responsiveness:** This entails a commitment to equity and cultural responsiveness. According to educator Vernita Mayfield (2020), equity and cultural responsiveness involve rejecting practices that perpetuate marginalization and promoting practices that cultivate understanding, respect, and productive interaction among people from diverse backgrounds.

4. **Flexible assessment practices:** This emphasizes the importance of multiple opportunities and diverse formats for students to demonstrate their knowledge.

5. **Mastery-oriented instruction:** This centers the vision around progression and promotion based on students demonstrating that they have mastered the learning outcomes.

Schools and districts can also articulate a collective guiding vision around a set of beliefs. For example, Westminster Public Schools organized their vision around four core beliefs (Gotto et al., 2025).

1. Learning matters most (learning is the constant).
2. Time matters least (time is the variable).
3. Implementation is systemic and systematic (policy, process, and practice).
4. Delivery is personalized (learner driven).

Even after they had fully implemented competency-based practices, these core beliefs continued to guide their vision, ensuring that any new practice strengthened the system.

Once a school has centered its work around a collective guiding vision, it engages in the decision-making process described in chapters 1 through 7 of this book to select and customize competency-based practices aligned with that vision. Each chapter represents a domain of competency-based practices. To identify each of these domains, we analyzed the literature shown in table I.1 (page 13); each of the following domains deserves consideration from educators seeking to implement competency-based practices.

1. Structure and reporting
2. Student outcomes
3. Agency
4. Equity
5. Assessment
6. Instruction
7. Adult roles

These domains represent the areas in which schools must make decisions about the competency-based practices that will propel them toward their vision. The domains that a school addresses—and the practices it implements within each domain—determine the manifestation of a competency-based approach in that school. As with all change initiatives, it is crucial that the decision-making process involves members from all levels of the organization, including leaders, teachers, staff, and—when appropriate and they possess the expertise to understand the impact of the decisions—students and parents.

Once a school has selected the competency-based practices that it will implement and decided how each of those practices will manifest in the school, it is important that the school creates expectations and procedures to manage and monitor each practice and ensure that the practices work in harmony with one another. As we highlight throughout this book's chapters, the presence of a systems approach is often the difference between successful and unsuccessful efforts at implementing competency-based practices. In other words, once a school has decided which competency-based practices to implement, it will then need to establish agreed-on policies, structures, and procedures that support implementing those practices.

In This Book

The chapters of this book align with the seven domains produced by our analysis of the research and theory on competency-based practices. We recommend thinking of those domains in two categories—(1) structural domains and (2) procedural domains—and have organized the book into two parts accordingly. The first four domains are structural: They deal with what David Tyack and Larry Cuban (1995; Cuban, 2020) called the *grammar of schooling*—the unseen architecture that organizes what happens in schools. We address these four domains in part 1 of the book. The other three domains are procedural: They deal with instructional and measurement processes. We address the procedural domains in part 2 of the book.

In part 1, we begin with the first, and most important, structural domain: structure and reporting. The four structural domains are not created equal; decisions related to the first domain (structure and reporting) apply to the other three. In chapter 1, we discuss six scenarios for implementing competency-based practices in schools, emphasizing a gradual transition from basic changes to more significant shifts in educational structure. Each scenario outlines different methods for assessing and reporting student progress, ranging from offering overall grades for subjects with detailed tracking of specific learning outcomes to allowing students to advance based on demonstrated mastery of topics, ultimately prioritizing individual learning and continuous improvement.

Chapter 2 explores the idea that competency-based practices seek to integrate academic and nonacademic outcomes, recognizing the importance of skills like collaboration and self-regulation while managing curriculum demands through clearly defined expectations. Proficiency scales play a crucial role in this approach, providing structured, transparent pathways for students to achieve learning outcomes while also promoting a supportive and collaborative learning environment that enhances motivation and equity.

In chapter 3, we address student agency. Student agency goes beyond boosting self-esteem; it involves creating supportive environments where students can see their progress and feel a sense of control over their learning outcomes. This is achieved through intentional classroom designs that encourage initiative, promote student voice, provide choices, involve students in creating standard operating procedures, and emphasize the importance of reflection, ultimately enhancing motivation, engagement, and ownership of the learning process.

Chapter 4 discusses how to create competency-based schools that foster equity, encourage teachers to model inclusive practices, and help all stakeholders better understand one another's diverse values and beliefs. An equity-based approach, like most competency-based approaches, addresses individual needs, enhances cultural responsiveness, and empowers all students, while also emphasizing the importance of teacher quality and collaborative professional development to create inclusive and equitable educational environments.

Part 2 of the book focuses on the procedural domains, which address competency-based practices related to instructional and measurement processes. We consider these in a straightforward manner, beginning with the first procedural domain—assessment—in chapter 5. Assessment communicates the value of a learner's work and provides essential feedback for improvement; however, if assessments are not valid and reliable, they can mislead students and teachers. Effective assessment systems should focus on timely, detailed feedback and incorporate multiple assessment types, enabling flexibility and student engagement, while allowing teachers to synthesize formative scores into a summative score that accurately reflects a student's proficiency and progress over time.

Chapter 6 zeros in on instruction, focusing on ways teachers can facilitate student interaction with content and accommodate varied pacing, which requires thoughtful adjustments in planning and delivery. Competency-based practices often include project-based learning, small-group instruction, and blended learning, utilizing online resources alongside teacher support to enhance cognitive engagement and mastery. At the same time, competency-based instruction emphasizes continuous improvement through structured reviews and the use of proficiency scales to guide student progress.

Finally, chapter 7 emphasizes the need for educators in competency-based education systems to shift from traditional instructional roles to more facilitative positions, addressing challenges like vulnerability and resistance to change while fostering collaboration for enhanced professional learning and student outcomes. It highlights the importance of effective student groupings, flexible scheduling, advisory systems, and continuous professional development.

The shift to competency-based education is one of boundless possibilities, both in the potential benefits to students and in the ways a school might implement competency-based practices. In these pages, we consider the decision points that will help you develop the unique local system that ensures your students succeed.

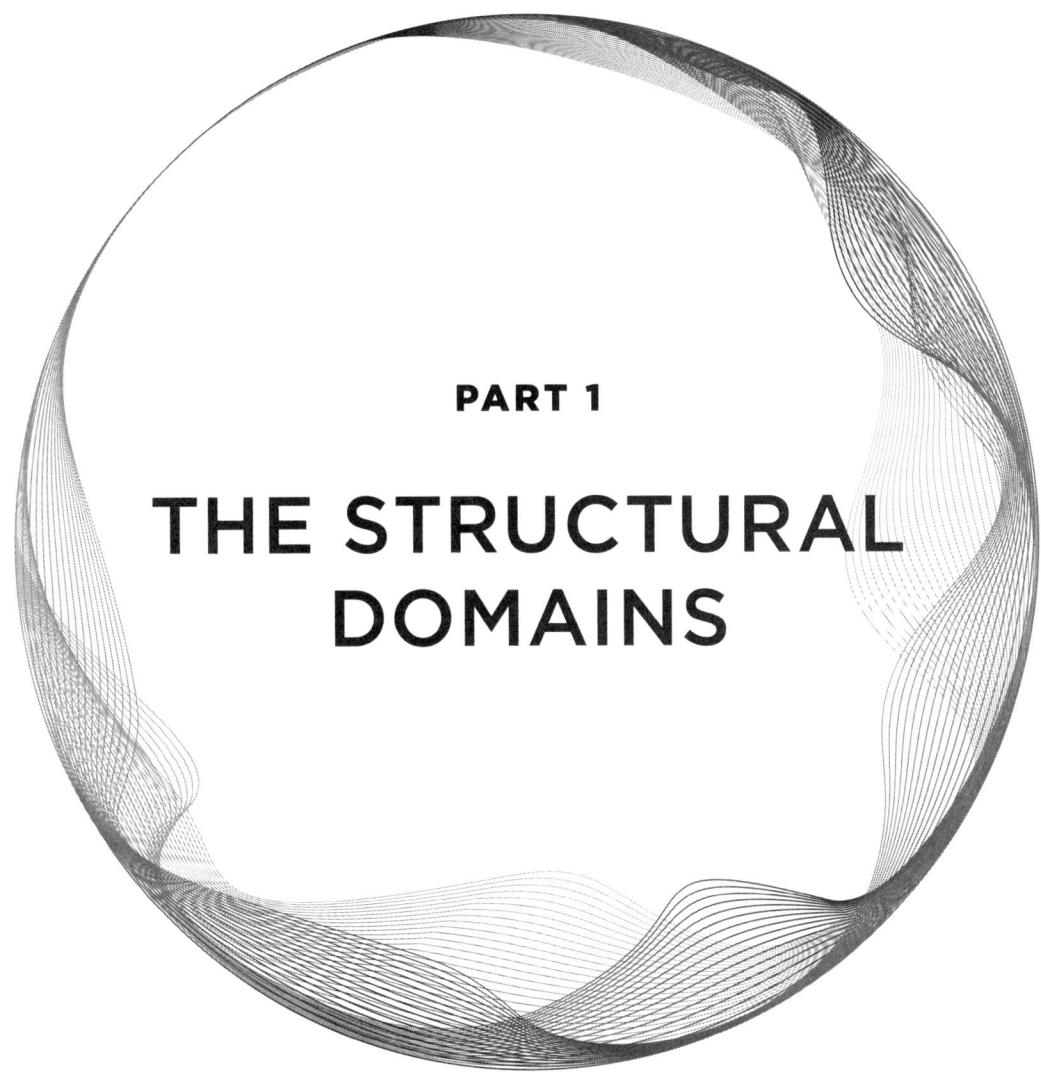

PART 1

THE STRUCTURAL DOMAINS

The four structural domains—(1) structure and reporting, (2) student outcomes, (3) agency, and (4) equity—work together to create a strong configuration of competency-based practices. While decisions in the first domain, structure and reporting, have a foundational impact on the other domains, each area requires its own set of critical decisions. In the structure and reporting domain, schools must determine how to integrate and report student performance, whether through an overall grade, individual outcomes, or mastery-based metrics. The student outcomes domain involves selecting categories of knowledge and skills that students are expected to master, determining how to structure these outcomes, and deciding how to articulate them for clarity. Agency focuses on giving students control over their learning by providing activities and support that foster self-efficacy while also considering how to measure agency-related outcomes. Finally, the equity domain requires schools to ensure that every student experiences fairness and inclusion by addressing social and cultural factors that impact success. Together, these domains form the backbone of a competency-based system, where decisions made in one area influence and support those in others, creating a cohesive and intentional approach to student learning and achievement.

CHAPTER 1

Structure and Reporting

The second wave of competency-based education (since 1989) shows great promise. However, it is threatened by one issue that educational psychologist William G. Spady (Spady, 1977, 1978; Spady & Mitchell, 1977) and others first identified in the 1970s. Competency-based education requires educators, students, and parents to rethink and retool what Tyack and Cuban (1995) called "the grammar of schooling" (p. 85; see also Cuban, 2020). That is, in order for students to receive adequate time and opportunity to learn the content, school structures—along with adult expectations, beliefs, and practices regarding those structures—need to change.

As schools implement competency-based practices, many of them dramatically change "customary school practice" (Tyack & Cuban, 1995, p. 85). For example, as highlighted by Marzano and colleagues (Marzano et al., 2019; Marzano & Abbott, 2022; Marzano & Hardy, 2023), changes to grading and reporting systems may contradict students' and parents' expectations about receiving overall letter grades, class rankings, and traditional transcripts. An even more extreme example involves implementing flexible pacing, which, according to Evans and colleagues (2019), "is one of the most difficult competency-based practices to implement" (p. 322). Grade levels and the concept that all students complete one grade per academic year are so entrenched in school systems that many people use grade levels as a verbal shortcut to communicate a student's age: "My fourth grader is tall for his age." Often, parents' memories of their own school experiences are tied to specific grade levels: "I started gymnastics in second grade," or "I played baseball my sophomore year." Uncoupling grade levels from specific ages significantly fractures the grammar of schooling.

Given the difficulty around changes to traditional schooling structures, we recommend that a school carefully consider the order in which it makes these changes. For example, beginning by implementing flexible pacing has the potential to disrupt several school structures all at once. There are programs and practices that need to be in place prior to the effective movement of students based on mastery. Without them, decisions about why and when a student changes classes or levels may not be clear and can lead to confusion for students, teachers, and parents. For example, Westminster Public Schools made an early move from the traditional thirteen grade levels to ten performance levels. Parents struggled to understand whether their student was ahead or behind, so Westminster Public Schools eventually aligned their performance levels with traditional grade levels, making the change to flexible pacing easier for parents to accept (Gotto et al., 2025).

A school can begin with whatever scenario best suits its current situation. By moving through the scenarios in a logical and linear way, stakeholders have time to get used to new procedures and new expectations one step at a time. In fact, stakeholders may even discover for themselves the necessity for the next step once previous steps are in place. The six scenarios are as follows.

1. **Teach outcomes but report overall grade:** Classroom instruction and assessment are organized around individual outcomes, but teachers report only one overall grade or score for each subject area.

2. **Teach and report outcomes:** Classroom instruction and assessment are organized around individual outcomes, and teachers report students' scores for each individual outcome with the option of having an overall grade or score for the course or level.

3. **Allow students the opportunity to raise previous scores:** If a student is not pleased with their current score for a particular outcome, they can take action to increase that score, even after the end of an instructional unit or grading period.

4. **Require mastery of some outcomes:** Students must master a selected set of outcomes for each level of each subject area to move to the next level.

5. **Require mastery of all outcomes:** Students must master all outcomes for each level of each subject area to move to the next level.

6. **Allow students to move at a mastery pace:** Students who have mastered all the outcomes for a level of a subject area immediately advance to the next level, regardless of time.

Important grading and reporting ramifications accompany each of these scenarios. Table 1.1 summarizes the implications of these decisions for grading and reporting.

Table 1.1: Implications for Grading

	Implication	Overall Grade or Score	Individual Outcome Scores	Cumulative Approach to Grading	Overall Pace
1	Teach outcomes but report overall grade	✓			
2	Teach and report outcomes	✓	✓		
3	Allow students the opportunity to raise previous scores	✓	✓	✓	
4	Require mastery of some outcomes	✓	✓	✓	
5	Require mastery of all outcomes	✓	✓	✓	
6	Allow students to move at a mastery pace		✓	✓	✓

It's important to note a commonality across each of these scenarios, including scenario 1 (which is most closely aligned to the traditional grammar of schooling). Each scenario presupposes that teachers are directly teaching and assessing specific learning outcomes and reporting student performance on the learning outcomes as accurately as possible, and they are not using practices that interfere with that endeavor. For example, teachers do not award students points for activities that are not directly related to specific learning outcomes (such as bringing extra supplies to class, getting a syllabus signed, or turning in work on time) or take away points for infractions (such as turning in work late or putting their name in the wrong corner of the assignment). Therefore, as a prerequisite to making decisions for domain 1, a school must address any of these practices that are being used. There are several ways to help teachers navigate this transition. One option is to create life-skills learning outcomes that include criteria like "Collaboration With Peers" and "On-Time Assignment Completion." You could also introduce an "M" or "Missing" score for any assignments not turned in or submitted late (for additional ideas, see Flygare, Hoegh, & Heflebower, 2022; Heflebower, Hoegh, Warrick, & Flygare, 2019; and Hoegh, Flygare, Heflebower, & Warrick, 2023). These types of scoring options allow teachers to communicate how the student is performing as a learner without misrepresenting their academic achievement related to the learning outcomes. For schools that have met this prerequisite, the following sections on the six different scenarios will help you identify where to begin.

Scenario 1: Teach Outcomes but Report Overall Grade

In this scenario, a school directly teaches and assesses the various learning outcomes it has identified as important, but it does not report a score for each learning outcome. Instead, student performance on all learning outcomes within a subject area is integrated into an overall grade or score that is reported.

Here, and throughout the book, we use the term *measurement topics* to refer to the learning outcomes that each student is expected to learn at each level for each subject area. As defined by Robert J. Marzano and Patrick Hardy (2023), a measurement topic is "a specific topic within a subject area that teachers will teach, assess, and score students on" (p. 41). The use of the term *measurement* in this label is intentional, as these topics form the ultimate basis and foundation for classroom assessments that measure students' current status on specific knowledge or skills (Marzano, 2018). And, as we will explain in chapter 2 (page 39), we highly recommend that a learning progression, or *proficiency scale*, be articulated for each measurement topic. Because the proficiency scales we describe in chapter 2 involve a scale for scores ranging from 0.0 to 4.0 (with 3.0 representing proficiency), examples in this chapter and throughout the book will often refer to students' scores within that range.

In this first scenario, teachers focus their instruction and assessment on individual outcomes articulated as measurement topics. A teacher in this scenario might even organize a gradebook by outcomes and keep track of a series of scores for each student on each outcome. However, when a teacher reports student status at the end of each grading period (whether semester, trimester, or six-week period), the teacher simply reports one grade or score—often called an *omnibus grade*—to represent that student's status in that subject area.

This overall grade or score will not provide any detail about specific outcomes with which the student either excels or struggles. Indeed, the focus of this scenario is on giving teachers time to learn and internalize how to organize instruction, assessment, and tracking student progress on individual outcomes. If teachers do not have the time and support to understand how to do this before being asked to report on individual outcomes (as in the next scenario), their lack of comfort and familiarity can hinder (and has the potential to derail) all subsequent scenarios.

For example, an ELA teacher teaches and assesses students on specific learning outcomes such as analyzing narratives, evaluating claims, and generating sentence structure; each of these constitutes one measurement topic. Daily lessons align with these topics, and the teacher monitors students' progress on these topics using assessments. However, when the teacher reports scores at the end of a reporting period, the scores on each measurement topic are combined—most likely as an average—into one score for each student.

As another example, the science teachers in a school have identified measurement topics for seventh grade. They have also determined the order in which they will teach the topics and how long they will spend on each, such as "in seventh-grade science, we will teach the measurement topic of human energy for fifteen to eighteen days at the beginning of the academic year." As they teach each topic, the teachers record scores for each student over the course of time allocated to this topic. Then they administer an end-of-topic assessment toward the end of the allocated time and decide to what extent each student has acquired the knowledge and skills encompassed in the human energy topic. Figure 1.1 shows how this might look for one student after the first marking period (in which three topics were taught).

Topic	Score 1	Score 2	Score 3	Score 4	Score 5	Final Score
Human Energy	2.0	2.0	2.0	3.0	3.0	3.0
Force, Energy, and Motion	2.0	3.0	3.0	3.0	3.0	3.0
Electricity	1.0	2.0	2.0	2.0	2.0	2.0
Final Score (average of final scores)						2.66

Figure 1.1: Scores for a student on three science measurement topics.

As figure 1.1 shows, although the teacher tracked a series of scores for this student for each measurement topic and assigned a final score to the student for each measurement topic, only one final score—2.66, which is the average of the final scores from each of the three measurement topics—is assigned for science at the end of the marking period.

Scenario 2: Teach and Report Outcomes

In this scenario, a school directly teaches and assesses the various learning outcomes identified as important and reports a score for each learning outcome. In addition to reporting scores for each learning outcome, the school integrates student performance on all learning outcomes within a subject area into an overall grade or score, which is reported along with the scores on individual measurement topics.

Ideally, teachers have already practiced grading students on individual outcomes in the previous scenario, but if not, they must begin tracking students' scores on individual outcomes at this stage. Teachers report student status at the end of each grading period *for each individual measurement topic* addressed during the marking period. The ELA section of a report card for this type of reporting might look as shown in figure 1.2; the full report card would include similarly detailed sections for all the subjects shown in the summary section at the top.

Notice in figure 1.2 that there are bars representing the student's current status on each outcome. Each bar has a dark section and a lighter section. This is a convenient way to report student growth on each outcome, and we highly recommend that the school report both growth and status when they make the shift from reporting an omnibus grade to reporting on individual outcomes. Marzano and colleagues (2019) further explained the graphing as follows:

> *Of particular importance is the dark part of each bar graph in comparison to the light part. This area depicts growth, since the dark part of the graph is the student's first score and the light part is the student's current summative score. (p. 105)*

It is important to note that while this scenario requires teachers to collect and record scores only on measurement topics, some teachers may wish to collect data on nonacademic factors such as work completion, classroom behavior, and the like. This is not a problem, but nonacademic data must be kept separate from the measurement topic scores (Marzano et al., 2017).

Grade Level: 5

Language arts	2.56	B−
Mathematics	3.18	A−
Science	2.56	B−
Social studies	2.94	B+
Art	2.75	B

Generating conclusions	2.70	B
Navigating digital sources	3.50	A
Staying focused	3.00	A−
Seeking accuracy	3.00	A−

		0.5	1.0	1.5	2.0	2.5	3.0	3.5	4.0
English Language Arts									
Decoding	2.5								
Analyzing text organization and structure	1.5								
Analyzing ideas and themes	2.0								
Analyzing claims	3.5								
Analyzing narratives	2.5								
Comparing texts	1.0								
Analyzing words	2.5								
Generating text organization and structure	3.0								
Generating sentence structure	3.0								
Generating claims	3.0								
Using citations	2.5								
Generating narratives	2.5								
Generating point of view and purpose	3.0								
Writing for a specific audience	3.0								
Using specific words and parts of speech	3.0								
Punctuation, capitalization, and spelling	2.0								
Revision and editing	3.0								

Average for English Language Arts: 2.56

Source: Marzano et al., 2017, p. 162.
Figure 1.2: Report card for individual outcomes.

Scenario 3: Allow Students the Opportunity to Raise Previous Scores

In the previous scenario, students did not have the option to change their scores once they were reported. At the end of each grading period, the teacher reports student status (and ideally growth) on each outcome, and that score stands, unless the teacher further addresses the outcome and raises student scores (as might be the case if a measurement topic was not fully taught within a grading period). In contrast, students in scenario 3 have the opportunity for continuous score improvement. If a student receives a score that is lower than they want, they have the opportunity to provide further evidence of their learning. If the teacher agrees that the student's actual score is now higher than the one previously recorded, the teacher increases the student's recorded score for that topic. For example, a student could complete an independent project or independent study with a plan for deepening their understanding of the content and then request a review from their teacher. If the teacher agrees that the student's actual score for that outcome is higher than what the student previously demonstrated, the teacher immediately raises the student's score to the appropriate level.

In each new grading period, the teacher introduces new measurement topics, which are added to the report card. If using an overall grade, the student's score would be based on the new measurement topics as well as those already covered in the course or level. Additionally, teachers would provide students with opportunities to demonstrate an increase in their current status on previously scored measurement topics (Marzano, 2018). For example, in a seventh-grade science classroom, a student's score at the end of the first marking period for the measurement topic of Newton's laws of motion was a 2.5. During the second marking period, while working on the measurement topic of gravity, the student acquires new knowledge that gives them fresh insight into Newton's laws of motion. The student drafts an explanation to demonstrate their understanding of the connection between gravity and Newton's laws of motion. As a result, the teacher changes the student's score for the topic of Newton's laws of motion from a 2.5 to 3.0.

As another example, an ELA student was unable to demonstrate mastery (that is, score 3.0 or higher) for the measurement topic of generating narratives by the end of the first semester. During the second semester, the student continues to practice narrative writing and drafts a personal narrative several weeks into the semester. The teacher reads the student's narrative and determines that the student has mastered the measurement topic of generating narratives. Even though that measurement topic is not being formally taught during the second semester, the teacher updates the student's score to reflect mastery of the measurement topic.

Figure 1.3 shows another way to conceptualize this scenario. In the figure, a team of third-grade teachers has identified the ELA measurement topics they will teach and report in each quarter of the academic year. Students are invited to continue to improve their score on a measurement topic in any quarter following the opportunity to learn that topic.

Third-Grade ELA Measurement Topics	Quarter 1	Quarter 2	Quarter 3	Quarter 4
Ask and Answer Questions				✓
Determine Central Message			✓	✓
Describe Character	✓	✓	✓	✓
Compare and Contrast Texts			✓	✓
Determine Main Idea		✓	✓	✓
Use Text Features	✓	✓	✓	✓
Identify Author's Point of View		✓	✓	✓
Determine Text Structure			✓	✓
Generate Opinion Writing	✓	✓	✓	✓
Generate Informational Writing		✓	✓	✓

Figure 1.3: Measurement topics to teach and report during each quarter of the academic year.

Scenario 3 raises a philosophical question for schools: After a measurement topic is taught and assessed, should a student who wants to improve be given one, two, or unlimited opportunities to do so? Historically, students have typically been given a single opportunity to demonstrate their knowledge or ability on a particular topic. Once the student has turned in an assignment or taken the assessment, the student's score is the final grade. However, if a school adopts a different philosophical approach—removing time-based constraints on student learning—it opens new possibilities. In this scenario, the school values learning over time, embracing the idea that time is variable and learning is constant. In other words, mastery of a topic is the highest priority, even if it takes a student more time or additional opportunities. We believe this approach is the right one for education, although it requires a significant shift from traditional practices.

Scenario 4: Require Mastery of Some Outcomes

In all previous scenarios, students continue to advance through grade levels based largely on their age. That is to say, even if a student hasn't mastered all the outcomes for third grade by the end of the year, they are still likely to progress to fourth grade. Scenario 4 begins to break that school structure by requiring students to demonstrate mastery of a selected set of outcomes before they are allowed to move to the next grade level. Notice that we are careful to say *a selected set of outcomes*; identifying a subset of outcomes for which mastery is required before progressing to the next level is a logical way of beginning to break the age-based criterion for movement through the grade levels. Teachers would still teach, assess, and report on each of the remaining measurement topics as described in scenario 2, but students would not be expected to demonstrate learning at the mastery level.

We strongly encourage schools to begin the move toward requiring mastery with this type of gradual approach, given the potentially large-scale impacts of requiring mastery on all topics too quickly. For example, Robert J. Marzano, Jennifer S. Norford, Michelle Finn, and Douglas Finn III (2017) described some of the ramifications of rushing toward requiring mastery on all topics:

> One of the most important factors a district or school must consider . . . is how quickly they wish to implement the rule that every student must achieve proficiency on each measurement topic before moving on to the next level. **Implementing this rule too quickly can send shock waves through a system.**
>
> To illustrate, assume that a high school has decided that all students must show proficiency in all measurement topics before they can move to the next course. For seniors, this could mean that many students do not graduate on time since they previously have not been required to meet such high expectations. Indeed, in the past, the graduation requirements were credit based, which meant that students only had to pass a certain percent of courses. (p. 171, emphasis added)

When Westminster Public Schools reached this scenario in their competency-based implementation, they created reasonable expectations for high school students who were close to graduation. Rather than requiring mastery of all high school topics for current high school students, the district decided to require mastery of 80 percent of a course's measurement topics before advancing to the next level (Gotto et al., 2025).

It is important to note that, while an overall grade can still be assigned in this scenario, it will begin to have less variation across students. Requiring mastery on some outcomes will narrow the variation because all students will be required to achieve a specific score on certain outcomes, whereas previously a student might have progressed to the next grade level without achieving that score on any outcomes. This narrowing of the variation in overall grades becomes much more pronounced in the next scenario.

Scenario 5: Require Mastery of All Outcomes

In this scenario, students are required to master all the outcomes at a particular level for a particular subject area before moving on to the next level for that subject area. As noted previously, requiring mastery on every outcome means that students' overall grades for each level and subject area will narrow. Marzano and Hardy (2023) described this reduction in grade variation as follows:

> *If the cut score for the grade of A starts at an average score of 3.0, then ultimately, every student will obtain a letter grade of A by the time they finish a course. There is clearly nothing wrong with this outcome. However, some secondary schools choose to establish different cut points for the traditional letter grades such that all students will not automatically receive an A when they have demonstrated proficiency on the scales. (pp. 66-67)*

For example, at the secondary level, a school might choose to set the cut score for the grade of A at 3.5 instead of 3.0. Thus, to achieve a grade of A, students would have to achieve a score of 4.0 on at least half of the measurement topics in a level. As Marzano and Hardy (2023) stated, "The higher the cut score for a grade of A, the more scores of 4.0 are needed to achieve it. Accordingly, the cut score for the grade of B is also much higher, and so on" (p. 67). If you think it seems somewhat arbitrary for schools or districts to set the cut scores for grades as described here, remember that the current grading system where an A is matched to a 90–100 percent and a B to a 80–89 percent might be considered equally arbitrary; in most cases, the best choice is a system created by and agreed on among all stakeholders in a school or district.

It is also important to note that, in this scenario, students who achieve mastery on all the measurement topics for a level in a subject area do not immediately move to the next level. They might complete independent projects or enrichment or extension activities if they have already demonstrated proficiency on all the measurement topics for their current level. Because that particular change is saved for the next scenario, overall grades can still be reported in this scenario, albeit with much less variation than previous scenarios.

Scenario 6: Allow Students to Move at a Mastery Pace

In this scenario, students are allowed to move ahead when they have demonstrated mastery of all measurement topics within their current level or course regardless of the time they have spent in that level or course. For example, if a ten-year-old student demonstrates mastery in all the measurement topics for fifth-grade science, they move on to sixth-grade science measurement topics immediately, without waiting for the end of the school year. This might mean that the student's schedule changes to accommodate their participation in a different science class. Alternatively, the student's schedule might stay the same, but their current teacher is empowered to teach and assess sixth-grade science measurement topics with this student. In another example, if there are fifteen measurement topics associated with Algebra I and a student demonstrates mastery of all fifteen topics, the student immediately moves to the next course (likely either Geometry or Algebra II, depending on the school's mathematics course progression). Thus, students in this scenario will likely be working at varying levels depending on the subject area. A nine-year-old student might be working on sixth-grade mathematics and third-grade ELA. This is a normal outcome of implementing scenario 6.

In this scenario, reporting an overall grade for each subject area becomes impractical and essentially useless. It is much more effective to report grades using pace. That is, instead of reporting an overall grade that summarizes a student's performance across outcomes for their age-based grade, the school reports a pace metric that summarizes how many levels and outcomes a student has demonstrated mastery on for that subject area. A student might have demonstrated mastery on all the mathematics outcomes for grades K, 1, and 2, and on half the outcomes for grade 3. Therefore, their pace metric for mathematics would be 2.5. This could be compared to their age to determine whether they are moving at an appropriate pace. If a student has a 2.5 in mathematics and is seven years old, they are probably on pace. If a student is five years old, they are ahead of pace, and if they are nine, they are behind pace.

At the high school level, this scenario will likely require adjustments to transcripts. According to the Education Policy Innovation Collaborative (2021), schools implementing competency-based practices in this scenario usually do the following:

> *Adjust how they give grades and transcripts to students. . . . This may include alternative transcripts with lists of skills students have mastered rather than traditional grades. It may also include efforts to standardize grading practices across grades or content areas. (p. 14)*

The change represented by scenario 6 has the potential to yield more productive and meaningful credentials for students and could also correct many of the shortcomings of the current high school transcript or diploma based on seat time. Susan Patrick, Natalie Truong, and Alexis Chambers (2020) elaborated on this change:

> *There is wide variability in preparedness by students who hold a diploma; it signals very little about what they know and can do.*
>
> *A more meaningful high school credential would focus on the knowledge, skills, and competencies based on demonstrated mastery, rather than on seat-time.* (p. 8)

Figure 1.4 (page 38) presents one example of a pace-based progress report for a high school student.

Another practical consideration for schools implementing scenario 6 is to communicate concepts related to pace. In the early stages of implementing competency-based education in Westminster Public Schools, the phrase "at the student's pace" often led to misunderstandings; were students allowed to go as fast or as slow through the content as they wanted? The district had to clarify that the teacher sets the pace, particularly for students who are behind or have gaps in their learning (Gotto et al., 2025).

At its best, scenario 6 can lead to many unanticipated celebrations, such as early graduation—a phenomenon that is relatively rare in most traditional systems. In Westminster Public Schools, the number of early graduates has increased each year since 2013. Conversely, scenario 6 might lead a school to organize a second, smaller graduation ceremony (typically about a month after the regular graduation) to allow some students the bit of extra time they need to meet targets and fill remaining gaps.

Summary

In this chapter, we explored six scenarios that represent the structure and reporting decisions that a school must make as they implement competency-based practices. We addressed the desirability of beginning with less radical changes and gradually moving toward those that break the grammar of schooling in significant ways. On one end of the spectrum, with scenario 1, teachers have time to become proficient in tracking student progress at the measurement topic level before being required to report on it. On the other end of the spectrum, scenario 6 describes a context in which students progress to the next level in a subject as soon as they demonstrate mastery of all the measurement topics at their current level, regardless of age or school year. In the next chapter, we zoom in on student outcomes and examine the decisions that schools make about the knowledge and skills that students will master and how to articulate those in ways that clearly communicate expectations to all stakeholders.

38 | MARZANO MASTERY APPROACHES

Absences:	15		Tardies:	25	
Pacing			**Eligibility**		**Missing Work (last thirty days)**
Physics	On Pace		Physics		Physics	0
College Algebra	Behind Pace		College Algebra		College Algebra	0
IB Spanish SL1	Behind Pace		IB Spanish SL1		IB Spanish SL1	0
U.S. History	Behind Pace		U.S. History		U.S. History	0
ELA 3	Behind Pace		ELA 3		ELA 3	2
Athletic Team Fitness 2			Athletic Team Fitness 2		Athletic Team Fitness 2	0
Academic Enrichment	Behind Pace		Academic Enrichment	3.0	Academic Enrichment	0

Physics — Teacher Name — On Pace

Student's progress	96%
Expected progress	78%
Missing work	0
Eligibility	
Work habits	
Earned credit	0.5 Credit (First Half Credit)
Final course score	3.0 (Date)

IB Spanish SL1 — Teacher Name — Behind Pace

Student's progress	10%
Expected progress	78%
Missing work	0
Eligibility	
Work habits	
Earned credit	0.5 Credit (First Half Credit)
Final course score	3.0 (Date)

College Algebra — Teacher Name — Behind Pace

Student's progress	58%
Expected progress	78%
Missing work	0
Eligibility	
Work habits	
Earned credit	0.5 out of 1.0
Final course score	

U.S. History — Teacher Name — Behind Pace

Student's progress	0%
Expected progress	78%
Missing work	0
Eligibility	
Work habits	
Earned credit	0.5 out of 1.0
Final course score	

Source: © 2024 by *Empower Learning, LLC*. Used with permission.
Figure 1.4: Example of a pace-based progress report.

CHAPTER 2

Student Outcomes

While early competency-based theorists used varying definitions and terminology for student outcomes (for example, Block, 1978; Spady & Mitchell, 1977), educators have mainly settled on the idea that *academic student outcomes* are largely drawn from standards documents (for example, see Colby, 2017). However, academic student outcomes are not the only knowledge that students need to learn in school. According to researcher Sarah Jenkins (2020), *nonacademic student outcomes*, such as collaboration, communication, self-regulation, and so on, "enable students to be successful in a variety of settings" and "can be broad enough to include the educational hopes and values of students from different racial, ethnic, ability and socioeconomic backgrounds" (p. 4). A school or district's nonacademic outcomes are often described in documents such as graduate profiles (also called *portrait of a graduate* or similar; Education Policy Innovation Collaborative, 2021; Patrick et al., 2020).

As conveyed in the introduction, adding nonacademic outcomes to the abundance of academic outcomes has the potential to exacerbate the standards movement's enduring problem: too much content. Therefore, schools that are implementing competency-based practices must protect their curriculum by being intentional and clear about exactly what content students are expected to learn at each level for each subject area. This endeavor is central to what Marzano (2003) called a *guaranteed and viable curriculum*. According to Marzano and Hardy (2023):

> *Guaranteed* means that the school ensures every teacher addresses a consistent set of topics articulated in a course of study.
>
> *Viable* means that the curriculum is focused and streamlined enough that teachers have time in the school day and in the school year to adequately teach and reinforce the content. (p. 42)

To ensure that curriculum is both guaranteed and viable, schools must carefully select the categories for which they will explicitly articulate expected outcomes. That is, for which *academic* areas will the school have expected outcomes, and what, if any, *nonacademic* outcomes will the school identify—whether cognitive skills, metacognitive skills, or self-system skills? (We will distinguish among these skills categories later in the chapter.)

For each category of expected outcomes, the school must select a structure and reporting approach. Recall from chapter 1 (page 25) that we articulated six different scenarios that a school might choose for structuring the instruction and reporting of learning outcomes. One of the benefits of considering academic and nonacademic outcomes separately is that it is possible (and often productive) to assign different structures and reporting scenarios to each. For example, if you chose, for academic outcomes, scenario 4 (that is, require mastery of some outcomes), you might, for nonacademic outcomes, choose scenario 2 (that is, teach and report outcomes). Using a less complex scenario for nonacademic outcomes can help reduce the complexity of reporting for teachers, students, and parents as they are getting used to a new structure of schooling.

For each category of expected outcomes, the school must also decide how they will articulate the outcomes. The goal for articulating student outcomes is transparency. *Transparency* means that what students learn is not up to the sole discretion of the teacher; instead, learning outcomes and expectations are agreed on before learning starts and clearly communicated to all stakeholders. Such transparency results in positive outcomes for students.

Specifically, research reported by Heather Hayes, Marylee Demeter, John G. Morris, and Goran Trajkovski (2021) found that when students know exactly what they are expected to learn and how they will be assessed on that learning, "the students internalize this information as self-directed goals" (p. 4). Haynes and colleagues (2016) reported that "having clear learning targets and requiring students to meet all learning targets to earn course credit in mathematics and ELA were both positively related to changes over time in intrinsic motivation" (p. 29). According to Marzano and Kosena (2022), the outcomes that students are expected to learn should be easily accessible and easily understood by everyone concerned in the educational endeavor. This includes students, parents and guardians, teachers, administrators, and "any other interested constituents within the community"

(Marzano & Kosena, 2022, p. 83). A transparent culture promotes empathy and connection and facilitates regular, clear, open, and collaborative conversations with students and their families. According to Mike Ruyle, Awachíikaate (Jason D. Cummins), Libby Child, and Donyall D. Dickey (2025), "Transparency can also be an effective tool in building trust and can help build higher levels of engagement, collaboration, and satisfaction, which can result in direct academic gains" (p. 62).

Consistent routines and transparent expectations are especially useful for students who experience poverty, trauma, or toxic stress, because predictable routines and reliable environments in classrooms can help balance the lack of safety and predictability they often encounter in their lives outside school (Ruyle et al., 2025). According to Hayes and colleagues (2021), "Transparency is achieved when students know (a) what is being assessed and (b) the criteria for good or acceptable performance" (p. 4). Having tried many of the available vehicles for promoting curricular transparency and observed others' use of those vehicles, we strongly recommend a specific approach, which we referred to briefly in the introduction (page 1) and chapter 1 (page 25), called *proficiency scales*.

Regardless of the approach you take toward implementing competency-based practices, the use of proficiency scales—or a similarly detailed and organized structure for articulating learning outcomes—is critical. Without the clarity provided by a detailed learning progression, the assessment and feedback required to make competency-based practices effective and efficient are not possible. Because of this, this chapter begins with a deep dive into the use of proficiency scales—namely, in the context of academic standards and outcomes—before moving into a review of the nonacademic student outcomes schools might make transparent.

Academic Outcomes and Proficiency Scales

A *proficiency scale* shows "exactly what students need to know and how they will get there" (Marzano & Kosena, 2022, p. 2). The design of proficiency scales grew out of the research on learning progressions, and like learning progressions, a proficiency scale describes the discrete steps that students must take to achieve a learning outcome or demonstrate mastery of a measurement topic (Marzano, 2010; Marzano et al., 2017). Wenmoth and colleagues (2021) reinforced the idea that this level of detail must form the basis for articulating student outcomes in a system of competency-based practices: "Expect the curriculum to be designed around learning progressions" (p. 10). The format and uses of proficiency scales articulated in this book have been developed and refined in classrooms since 1996 (Marzano, 2000, 2006, 2010; Marzano et al., 2017; Marzano & Kendall, 1996).

Many confuse proficiency scales with rubrics or use the two terms interchangeably. This is a mistake; rubrics and proficiency scales are distinctly different. Rubrics are used specifically for assessments and often for just a single assessment or project. A proficiency scale is used across the learning process for goal setting, instructional planning, monitoring, multiple types of assessments, scoring, and reporting (Marzano et al., 2017; Marzano & Kosena, 2022). Figure 2.1 presents a generic proficiency scale.

Score 4.0	Advanced content
Score 3.0	Target content
Score 2.0	Simpler content necessary for proficiency
Score 1.0	With help, partial success with score 2.0 content and score 3.0 content
Score 0.0	Even with help, no success

Source: Marzano et al., 2017, p. 28.
Figure 2.1: Generic proficiency scale.

Figure 2.2 presents a proficiency scale for a fifth-grade science measurement topic.

Score 4.0	The student will: Solve an engineering problem involving decisions about which material, based on its properties, will best satisfy a set of requirements and constraints.
Score 3.5	In addition to score 3.0 performance, partial success at score 4.0 content
Score 3.0	The student will: Classify materials based on their properties (magnetism, conductivity, density, solubility, boiling point, melting point).
Score 2.5	No major errors or omissions regarding score 2.0 content, and partial success at score 3.0 content
Score 2.0	The student will: Recognize and recall basic vocabulary, such as *boiling point*, *conductivity*, *density*, *magnetism*, *melting point*, and *solubility*. The student will perform basic processes, such as: • Make observations to identify the properties of a material. • Take measurements to identify the properties of a material.
Score 1.5	Partial success at score 2.0 content, and major errors or omissions regarding score 3.0 content
Score 1.0	With help, partial success at score 2.0 content and score 3.0 content
Score 0.5	With help, partial success at score 2.0 content but not at score 3.0 content
Score 0.0	Even with help, no success

Source: Marzano et al., 2017, p. 29.
Figure 2.2: Proficiency scale for properties of materials.

The starting point in constructing a proficiency scale is the score 3.0 content. This is the learning target that represents proficient performance with the target content at the specified level. This target does not need to be a direct copy of the standard language, as standards can be broad and may need to be broken down into smaller, manageable subgoals. Many educators we work with often say that "teaching to the standard does not mean teaching the standard." Next, the score 2.0 content represents simpler content related to the target content that the teacher will directly teach and assess. Finally, the score 4.0 content represents more complex content that goes beyond the target content and typically involves applying the target content in the real-world context of a knowledge application task. The descriptors for scores 1.0 and 0.0 do not change according to the topic of a proficiency scale. Half-point scores add a level of precision to proficiency scale–based scoring, which we will explore in more depth in chapter 5 (page 89).

While there is no single correct method for developing a proficiency scale, the following five steps are useful for developing a robust progression of knowledge for the 2.0, 3.0, and 4.0 levels of a proficiency scale.

1. Determine the topic of the proficiency scale.
2. Determine the language of score 3.0 (the target content).
3. Determine vocabulary related to the target content and record it at score 2.0.
4. Determine additional simpler content and record it at score 2.0.
5. Identify an example or two of how a student might demonstrate score 4.0 performance (the complex content).

For example, if a team of fourth-grade teachers is developing a proficiency scale for the ELA outcome "Refer to details and examples in a text when explaining what the text says explicitly and when drawing inferences from the text," (NGA & CCSSO, 2010a, RL.4.1), then they could use the five steps to produce a proficiency scale such as the one in figure 2.3 (page 44).

Marzano and colleagues (2019) described the following mistakes that educators sometimes make when constructing proficiency scales.

- **Referencing external criteria:** Statements such as "at the appropriate grade level" are not helpful in a proficiency scale because they don't identify the specific skills students need to exhibit to demonstrate proficiency.

Measurement Topic: Details and Examples in a Text	
Refer to details and examples in a text when explaining what the text says explicitly and when drawing inferences from the text.	
Score 4.0 Complex Content	The student will: • Suggest an additional detail or example that would strengthen an inference and defend their suggestion.
Score 3.0 Target Content	The student will: • Refer to details and examples in a text when explaining what the text says explicitly. • Refer to details and examples in a text when making inferences from a text. • Accurately answer text-provided inferential questions.
Score 2.0 Simpler or Foundational Content	The student will: • Recognize specific vocabulary such as *explicitly* and *inference*. • Use text details to answer "right there" or literal questions in a text. • Answer a question from the text without text evidence. • Make an inference without referring to text evidence.

Source for standard: NGA & CCSSO, 2010a, RL.4.1.
Figure 2.3: Progression of knowledge for the 2.0, 3.0, and 4.0 levels of a proficiency scale.

- **Using a generic scale for all measurement topics:** The power of a proficiency scale is in its specificity and description of the target, simpler, and more complex content.

- **Linking performance to behavioral consistency:** Descriptors such as *always, consistently, often, sometimes,* and *never* are problematic when trying to score a single assessment (a core function of proficiency scales); they apply only when examining a series of performances over time.

- **Including content from prior levels:** To provide teachers with clear guidance on their content responsibilities, it is essential that each level's content scale is distinct and does not overlap with other grade levels.

- **Including too much content:** When trying to determine whether students have reached proficiency, listing too many skills or understandings at any level of the scale muddies the water and reduces the usefulness of the scale.

As shown here, constructing a proficiency scale is fairly straightforward but requires a high level of engagement and decision making with the content to parse out individual learning targets from a standard statement and identify the most relevant foundational knowledge to teach. Because of the cognitive effort required to construct scales, many schools and districts opt to begin with a preexisting set of proficiency scales. For example, some states, such as Alabama, have created proficiency scales for their state standards in ELA, mathematics, science, and social studies (ALSDE Special Education Services, n.d.). Additionally, some organizations, such as Marzano Resources, have created sets of proficiency scales based on broad analyses of state and national standards (Dodson, 2019; Simms, 2016). Beginning with an established set of proficiency scales, where academic standards are already organized and articulated as learning progressions, provides a strong foundation for the next critical steps in proficiency scale adoption. Once proficiency scales are created, educators must adapt them to ensure student understanding, decide how to use them during instruction, and be prepared to customize and revisit them to maximize their effectiveness.

Student-Friendly Language

For proficiency scales to result in maximum transparency and be maximally useful, students must be able to understand them. Proficiency scales are usually written initially for a teacher audience and are sometimes difficult for students—especially younger students—to understand. When this is the case, they need to be rewritten in student-friendly language. Since at least the 1980s, we've known that putting learning targets in students' own words increases their understanding of learning goals (Knowles, 1980). You can do this student-friendly language translation yourself, or you can guide students as they do it. Robert J. Marzano, Alexander S. Aschoff, and Ashley Avila (2022) recommended the following:

> *When adapting the scales in this way, it is important to not dilute or oversimplify the material but rather reduce the linguistic complexity by shortening sentences, removing unnecessary material, using more familiar words, and using grammar that is more easily understood. Student-friendly scales can also include pictures or diagrams. (p. 12)*

Figure 2.4 (page 46) presents an example of a teacher version and a student-friendly version of the same proficiency scale. Notice how the developers adapted the language to increase their students' ability to engage successfully with the scale. Keep in mind that teachers should continue to use the teacher version of the scale for instruction and assessment; its more complex language and syntax often communicate nuances in the content that the adults providing instruction must keep in mind.

	Teacher Version	Student-Friendly Version
4.0	The student will: Identify and name non-unit fractions of a whole partitioned into two, three, or four equal portions. For example, when given a circle partitioned into four equal portions with two portions shaded, describe the shaded portions as both "one-half" and "two-fourths" of the circle.	I can say the fraction that is shown when someone divides a shape into two, three, or four equal parts and shades in at least two of them. For example, when someone gives me a circle divided into four equal parts with two of the parts shaded, I can say that "one-half" or "two-fourths" of the circle has been shaded.
3.5	In addition to score 3.0 performance, partial success at score 4.0 content	I can do all the things at level 3.0, and I can do some of the things at level 4.0.
3.0	The student will: **F1—Identify equal portions of partitioned two-dimensional figures.** For example, when given a set of identical two-dimensional figures that have been partitioned in various ways with one portion shaded, match those figures that have equal portions shaded.	**F1—I can pick out equal portions across shapes that have been divided into smaller parts.** For example, when someone gives me a set of identical shapes each divided into smaller parts in different ways with one part shaded in, I can pick out which shapes have a shaded part that covers the same amount of space as the shaded part of another shape.
2.5	No major errors or omissions regarding score 2.0 content, and partial success at score 3.0 content	I can do all the things at level 2.0, and I can do some of the things at level 3.0.
2.0	**F1—**The student will recognize or recall specific vocabulary (for example, *circle, equal portions, fourth, half, partition, quarter, rectangle, third, whole*) and perform basic processes such as: • Explain that equal portions of a whole shape will each cover the same amount of space. • Partition a given circle or rectangle into two, three, or four equal portions. • Partition the same shape into the same number of equal portions in different ways. For example, partition a rectangle into fourths by dividing it vertically into four equal columns, then partition a copy of the same rectangle into fourths by dividing it in half both vertically and horizontally to produce four smaller rectangles. • Describe a whole shape partitioned into equal portions as the composition of those portions. For example, when given a circle that has been partitioned into four equal portions, describe the whole circle as being equal to "four-fourths."	**F1—**I know what certain words mean (for example, *circle, equal portions, fourth, half, partition, quarter, rectangle, third, whole*) and can do things such as: • Explain that any equal parts of a whole shape will each cover the same amount of space. • Divide a circle or rectangle into two, three, or four equal parts. • Divide a shape into the same number of equal parts in different ways. For example, I can divide a rectangle into four equal parts by dividing it vertically into four columns or by dividing it vertically and horizontally to make four smaller rectangles. • Use fraction names to say how a shape that has been divided into equal parts is made up of all those parts together. For example, when someone gives me a circle that has been divided into four equal parts, I can describe the circle as being made up of "four-fourths" of the circle.

	Teacher Version	Student-Friendly Version
1.5	Partial success at score 2.0 content, and major errors or omissions regarding score 3.0 content	I can do some of the things at level 2.0 and at level 3.0.
1.0	With help, partial success at score 2.0 content and score 3.0 content	I can do some of the things at level 2.0 and at level 3.0 with help.
0.5	With help, partial success at score 2.0 content but not at score 3.0 content	I can do some of the things at level 2.0 with help.

Source: © 2021, 2023 by Marzano Resources. Used with permission.
Figure 2.4: Teacher and student-friendly versions of a proficiency scale for fractions.

When creating student-friendly proficiency scales, several key considerations should be kept in mind. First, when teachers create their own student-friendly versions of proficiency scales, it deepens their understanding of the standards they teach. Rewriting academic standards into language that students can easily understand requires teachers to engage with the standards in a more thoughtful way. This deeper understanding can lead to more intentional instruction toward clearer learning outcomes.

Second, student-friendly proficiency scales can go beyond just simplifying academic standards. They can be designed to include student self-assessment, aligned academic vocabulary, goal setting, progress tracking, and even self-reflection through student journaling. Other additions might include the following.

- Visual representations
- Examples of mastery
- Reflection prompts
- Growth mindset reminders
- Peer or teacher feedback sections
- Rewards (stickers or badges)
- Links to real-world applications
- Checkpoint dates
- Links to other closely aligned proficiency scales

These additional elements help students take ownership of their learning and engage more deeply with the material.

Instructional Use

Once teachers have created their proficiency scales, they have multiple options for using them. And use is important! We urge you to resist the temptation to introduce a proficiency scale at the beginning of a unit, post it on the board or wall, and then ignore it as the learning progresses. Robert J. Marzano and Seth D. Abbott (2022) explained that proficiency scales "should be a living, breathing part of daily life" in a classroom implementing competency-based practices (p. 12). Many teachers enlarge proficiency scales to poster size and track students' progress in real time using sticky flags or other markers. Others have students keep data binders or, for young students, tape proficiency scales to the tabletop or desktop. Additional ways to keep students engaged with proficiency scales include the following.

- **Common thread:** Make scales the centerpiece of instruction—the common thread that ties it all together. With students, explain, explore, reference, pick apart, reflect on, and even argue about the proficiency scale. Give each scale a nickname and use those nicknames—"Today we continue our work with the fractions scale"—so that students get used to them and activate relevant background knowledge when they hear them.

- **Self-administered preassessment:** When you initially introduce students to a scale, ask them to do an initial self-evaluation as you describe each skill. Much like breezing through an instruction manual to see all parts of the whole before working on a project, students should see all parts of the scale before beginning work toward its attainment so they understand "where we're going with this."

- **Part-to-whole discussion:** Help students understand that larger concepts and skills are composed of smaller concepts and skills. Use a building metaphor (such as using plastic building bricks) to explain that it is important to begin by putting all the little pieces together; you can't build a model with missing parts, and you can't magically make the whole model appear out of thin air.

- **Background knowledge awareness:** Use the proficiency scale to help students activate and assess what they already know about the measurement topic. To continue with the building metaphor, say, "Some of us are coming to this project with pieces of the model already built, and some of us have all the pieces scattered about the table and need extra help in finding just the right one."

Table 2.1 summarizes additional ways teachers commonly use a proficiency scale during instruction and assessment, with an example for each.

Table 2.1: Teacher Uses of Proficiency Scales

Use	Example
The teacher makes the proficiency scale accessible to all learners.	The proficiency scale is posted on the wall, included in the teacher's slide set, or provided to students in a three-ring binder or folder.
The teacher gives an overview of the proficiency scale for students at the beginning of a lesson.	Prior to teaching the content in the proficiency scale, the teacher gives an overview of each level for students, saying, "We are about to begin learning about citing textual evidence. By the end of the learning opportunity, the goal is for you to provide evidence of learning everything at score 3.0. To ensure this happens, I will also provide an opportunity for you to provide evidence of everything at score 2.0. Some of you may even go further than the target of score 3.0. That means you will provide evidence of learning the score 4.0 target."
The teacher asks students to explain the meaning of the levels on the proficiency scale.	The teacher pairs each student with a partner and asks one partner to explain the levels on a proficiency scale to the other partner. The other person listens for accuracy and offers additional information about the levels on the scale.
The teacher asks students to use the scale to explain a demonstration or experiment.	After presenting the demonstration or experiment, the teacher asks students to review the proficiency scale and find the parts of the scale that help explain the phenomena they just witnessed.
The teacher refers to the proficiency scale during a lesson.	The teacher indicates the learning target from the proficiency scale that is the focus of instruction by writing it on the whiteboard, putting a star by the learning target on the posted proficiency scale, or calling verbal attention to the relevant learning target.
The teacher helps students understand how assignments and activities relate to the proficiency scale.	At the end of a lesson, the teacher asks, "What did we address on the proficiency scale during this lesson?" A student might respond, "We addressed score 2.0 on the scale when learned about and practiced the vocabulary for this measurement topic."
The teacher asks students to reflect on the proficiency scale to determine their current level of performance.	At the end of a lesson, the teacher asks students to highlight everything on the scale they can show they've learned and invites students to self-assess their current score level based on what they highlighted.
The teacher assesses students on the learning targets from each level of the proficiency scale.	At the end of a lesson, the teacher administers an assessment to students that includes items from each level on the proficiency scale.

Source: Adapted from Hoegh, 2020.

Customization and Revision

Over time, you will need to engage with your proficiency scales in regular cycles of customization and revision. During these cycles of customization and revision, you should focus on the two following important tasks.

1. **Alignment:** Ensure alignment among the learning outcomes articulated in standards documents (intended curriculum), in the proficiency scales (taught curriculum), and in classroom, interim, and large-scale assessments (assessed curriculum; Marzano et al., 2024).
2. **Foundational skills:** Ensure that the foundational skills that teachers have agreed to directly teach and assess are clearly articulated at the 2.0 level of each proficiency scale.

These cycles of customization and revision, while regular, should not be overly frequent. It can be tempting to revise scales too often, especially when it becomes clear that an addition or deletion could enhance the design or when state academic standards change. However, redesigning scales—no matter how well intentioned—can have unintended consequences for both teachers and students. For example, adjusting the placement of a foundational skill from one grade level to another can disrupt continuity of learning for students; similarly, adjusting the wording or examples of target content can cause confusion and inconsistency among teachers. Such revisions should always be thoughtfully planned, executed, and communicated.

To prevent disruption, we recommend establishing a predetermined schedule for updating scales. For example, Westminster Public Schools reviews their proficiency scales once every five years (Gotto et al., 2025), although it might be more frequent for schools or districts in the initial stages of proficiency scale development. It is not uncommon in the first year or two to revisit the scales annually to respond to teacher feedback on using the scales during assessment and instruction in the classroom.

Nonacademic Outcomes

As highlighted at the beginning of this chapter, academic outcomes are not the only outcomes that are the focus of proficiency scales. Economists Anthony P. Carnevale and Nicole Smith (2013) of Georgetown University found that the following outcomes were among those in highest demand across all careers and occupations.

- Communication
- Leadership
- Problem solving and complex thinking
- Sales and customer service
- Teamwork

Educator Thomas Gauthier (2020) synthesized research by others (Eraut, 1994; Hora, 2016; Stokes, 2015) into a list of similarly in-demand employability skills.

- Collaboration
- Communication
- Contextual behavior
- Creativity
- Critical thinking
- Metacognition
- Motivation
- Problem solving
- Rational and organized thought process
- Self-efficacy

Using the term *habits of success* to describe nonacademic outcomes, researcher Eliot Levine (2021) noted that these habits "can be developed—they are not fixed, innate traits—but traditional approaches to K–12 education invest minimal effort in helping students develop them in explicit and deliberate ways" (p. 4). However, thanks to the increasing inclusion of these types of skills in standards documents, Marzano and Kosena (2022) noted that they are enjoying greater support among educational stakeholders and recommended that schools implementing competency-based practices make these skills "a formal part of the curriculum that is taught, reinforced, assessed, and reported" (p. 164). For example, table 2.2 (page 52) shows the nonacademic skills taught by Westminster Public Schools—which they call *personal relational competencies* (Gotto et al., 2025)—and the grade levels in which each is introduced and then reinforced.

Table 2.2 highlights an important consideration to keep in mind as you decide which nonacademic outcomes to include in your formal curriculum. Marzano and Kosena (2022) described the outcomes as follows:

> Not all [nonacademic] skills can nor should be taught at every grade level. Instead, the skills should be strategically assigned to individual teams to ensure consistency across the vertical progression of learning. . . . This is because each of the skills has a vertical progression of learning, gaining in complexity as students age. (p. 95)

Table 2.2: Personal Relational Competencies Taught in Westminster Public Schools

Domain	Personal Relational Competency	Grade Levels
Self-awareness	Emotional regulation	1, 4, 7
	Accurate self-perception	2, 5, 8
	Self-discipline	1, 4, 6
Self-management	Motivation and resilience	1, 4, 7
	Goal setting	2, 5, 8
	Self-advocacy	1, 4, 6
Relationship skills	Healthy relationships	1, 4, 6
	Teamwork	1, 4, 7
	Communication	2, 5, 8
Responsible decision making	Analysis and decision making	1, 4, 6
	Problem solving	2, 5, 8
	Evaluation and reflection	1, 4, 7
Social awareness	Empathy and compassion	1, 4, 6
	Cultural responsiveness	1, 4, 7
	Perspective taking	2, 5, 8

Source for domains: CASEL, 2020.

Specifically, nonacademic skills can be taught and assessed in grade bands, as described by Marzano and colleagues (2019):

> The expectations for [nonacademic] skills change and become more complex as students move up through the grade levels. However, they don't change that much from one grade level to another. Rather, it is more reasonable to assume that they have fewer levels of distinction. Thus, instead of designing different proficiency scales for each grade level, we recommend proficiency scales . . . for four grade-level bands: K–2, 3–5, 6–8, and 9–12. (p. 92)

In this book, we address nonacademic outcomes across three categories: (1) cognitive skills, (2) metacognitive skills, and (3) self-system skills.

Cognitive Skills

Cognitive skills can be divided into two categories: (1) cognitive analysis skills and (2) knowledge application skills. According to Marzano and Kosena (2022), *cognitive analysis skills* "are those that people use to analyze and dissect information so that they might understand it at deeper levels" (p. 92). Table 2.3 lists common cognitive analysis skills.

Table 2.3: Cognitive Analysis Skills

Cognitive Analysis Skill	Description
Comparing	*Comparing* is the process of determining similarities and differences between elements or concepts.
Analogical reasoning	*Analogical reasoning* is the process of determining how one set of elements or concepts relates to another set of elements or concepts.
Classifying	*Classifying* is the process of using definable attributes to organize concepts or elements into categories or related subcategories.
Analyzing perspectives	*Analyzing perspectives* is the process of analyzing one's own perspective and the reasoning supporting it and contrasting that with a different perspective and the reasoning supporting it.
Constructing support	*Constructing support* is the process of formulating a claim and then developing a well-constructed argument that supports it.
Analyzing errors in reasoning	*Analyzing errors* is the process of recognizing logical fallacies or errors in information generated by others or oneself.
Analyzing inferences	*Analyzing inferences* is the process of identifying the inferences one makes automatically and unconsciously as well as the inferences one makes during conscious reasoning.
Generating mental images	*Generating mental images* is the process of creating images that represent information and procedures.

Source: © 2017 by Marzano Resources. Adapted with permission.

According to Marzano and Kosena (2022), *knowledge application skills* "are typically employed when using knowledge in unique situations" (p. 92). Table 2.4 lists common knowledge application skills.

Table 2.4: Knowledge Application Skills

Knowledge Application Skill	Description
Decision making	*Decision making* is the process of generating and applying criteria to select between alternatives that appear equal.
Problem solving	*Problem solving* is the process of overcoming obstacles or constraints to achieve a goal.
Invention	*Invention* is the act of creating a new process or product that meets a specific identified need. In a sense, it is like problem solving in that it addresses a specific need. However, problem solving is limited in duration.
Experimental inquiry	*Experimental inquiry* is the process of generating a hypothesis about a physical or psychological phenomenon and then testing the hypothesis.

continued →

Knowledge Application Skill	Description
Investigation	*Investigation* is the process of identifying and then resolving differences of opinion or contradictory information about concepts, historical events, or future possible events.
Systems analysis	*Systems analysis* is the process of describing and analyzing the parts of a system with particular emphasis on the relationships among the parts.

Source: © 2017 by Marzano Resources. Adapted with permission.

Metacognitive Skills

At its simplest, *metacognition* is defined as thinking about thinking or awareness of one's own cognition (Marzano et al., 2019). More precisely, metacognitive skills are those used "to provide executive control over one's actions" (Marzano et al., 2017, p. 22). These skills are sometimes referred to as metacognitive tools (Costa, 2008) and, in other instances, as habits of mind (Costa & Kallick, 2009; Ennis, 1987, 1989, 2001; Paul, 1990). Marzano and Kosena (2022) explained that metacognitive skills "come into play when one is planning, setting goals, making decisions, reflecting, and so on" (p. 93). Table 2.5 lists common metacognitive skills.

Table 2.5: Metacognitive Skills

Metacognitive Skill	Description
Staying focused when answers and solutions are not immediately apparent	This skill helps students overcome obstacles and stay focused when challenges arise. It also helps students to recognize how much effort they are putting into accomplishing a specific task.
Pushing the limits of one's knowledge and skills	This skill helps students set goals and engage in tasks that are personally challenging. When using this skill, students will strive to learn more and accomplish more.
Generating and pursuing one's own standards for performance	This skill enables students to envision and articulate criteria for what a successful project will look like.
Seeking incremental steps	This skill helps students take on complex tasks using small incremental steps so they do not become overwhelmed by the task as a whole.
Seeking accuracy	This skill helps students vet sources of information for reliability and verify information by consulting multiple sources known to be reliable.
Seeking clarity	This skill helps students identify points of confusion when they are learning new information. This allows students to independently seek a deeper understanding.

Metacognitive Skill	Description
Resisting impulsivity	When faced with a desire to form a quick conclusion, this skill helps students refrain from doing so until they can gather more relevant information prior to taking action.
Seeking cohesion and coherence	When students are creating something with a number of interacting parts, this skill helps them monitor the relationships between what they are currently doing and the overall intent of the project in which they are engaged.
Setting goals and making plans	This skill helps students set short- and long-term goals, create timelines or blueprints, monitor progress, and make necessary adjustments.
Growth mindset thinking	This skill helps students take on challenging tasks with an attitude that helps them succeed, even when confronted by major obstacles.

Source: © 2017 by Marzano Resources. Adapted with permission.

As with cognitive skills, metacognitive skills need not be articulated at each individual grade level. Instead, a grade-banded approach is most appropriate. Marzano and colleagues (2019) described how expectations at each grade band might manifest:

> At the K–2 level, teachers expect students, when cued, to recognize when they are using a metacognitive skill. At grades 3–5, students can execute a simple version of the skill when teachers cue and guide them. At grades 6–8, students can independently recognize when they should use a specific metacognitive skill and execute a complex strategy relative to the skill. At grades 9–12, students can identify situations in and out of school in which they should use a metacognitive skill; they can use a personalized strategy they have developed; and they can examine the effectiveness of their actions. (p. 96)

Self-System Skills

Self-system skills include self-regulation, communication, collaboration, participation in a group, work completion, and behavioral regulation (Marzano & Abbott, 2022; Simms, 2024).

Self-system skills, in many ways, are baked into competency-based practices. For example, Marzano, Aschoff, and Avila (2022) observed that a competency-based system "requires students to exhibit self-regulation through activities such as conducting self-assessment, managing the time they take to work through the curriculum, and the like" (p. 161). While this may be true, there is still a need for teachers to provide guidance on acquiring self-system skills. Proficiency scales written for these skills help students understand the steps required to attain and refine these skills. Table 2.6 (page 56) lists common self-system skills.

Table 2.6: Self-System Skills

Self-System Skill	Description
Participation	*Participation* involves the set of decisions and actions that helps students add to group discussions and engage actively in questioning and answering questions.
Work completion	*Work completion* involves the set of decisions and actions that helps students manage their workload and complete tasks efficiently and effectively.
Behavior	*Behavior* involves the set of decisions and actions that helps students follow classroom rules and norms designed to create an efficient and orderly learning environment for all.
Working in groups	*Working in groups* involves the set of decisions and actions that helps students function as productive and supportive members of groups designed to enhance the learning of the students within those groups.

Source: © 2017 by Marzano Resources. Adapted with permission.

Considerations for Assessment

When creating proficiency scales for nonacademic skills, there are several considerations to keep in mind. Proficiency scales for cognitive skills follow the same format as scales for academic content, but—as mentioned previously—they would be differentiated in grade bands rather than at each individual grade level. The grade-band approach also applies to proficiency scales for metacognitive skills, but there is an additional wrinkle when constructing scales for metacognitive and self-system skills. Marzano and colleagues (2017) described scales for metacognitive and self-system skills as follows:

> *[They] have a slightly different logic from the proficiency scales for traditional content or cognitive skills. . . . [These] skills require some amount of learner will or volition. . . .*
>
> *For example, a student may understand that it is important to push the limit of one's knowledge and skill but rarely makes the decision to do so. Consequently, a proficiency scale for such a metacognitive skill would have to incorporate this volitional component. (p. 32)*

A student might exhibit strong metacognitive skills in one situation while not in another. For example, they are likely better able to seek clarity when they are not tired and possess the confidence to ask for help. If they recently had an experience that caused them to feel embarrassed, they might not be as comfortable asking for support. It is important that learners recognize that nonacademic outcomes, unlike many of the academic outcomes, can fluctuate. Rare is the person who can resist impulsivity in every moment of their life. Therefore, proficiency scales for nonacademic skills usually include targets that involve a student monitoring their levels of the nonacademic skill while engaged in learning, such as Westminster Public School's target within their emotional regulation proficiency scale: Recognizes own triggers to more complex emotions and uses strategies to address them in a healthy way.

This also means that metacognitive and self-system skills must be assessed using a situational approach, as described by Marzano and colleagues (2019):

> *Teachers might provide students with activities in which a particular metacognitive skill is necessary for success. For example, a teacher might give students a few brain-teaser problems to solve and remind them that they should use the metacognitive skill of staying focused when answers and solutions are not immediately apparent. Students would rate themselves after the exercise, and the teacher would engage them in a discussion of the metacognitive skill. The teacher would systematically engage students in activities like this and elicit their self-evaluations. He or she would also evaluate students based on observations. The teacher would then combine students' self-evaluation scores and observation scores to form estimates of summative scores. (p. 96)*

This approach differs from cognitive skills assessment, which typically happens within the context of an academic task.

Summary

Competency-based practices aim to balance academic and nonacademic outcomes by recognizing the importance of cognitive, metacognitive, and self-system skills alongside academic standards. Clearly defining learning targets using proficiency scales supports transparency in goal setting, instructional planning, assessment, and reporting. Translating those scales into student-friendly language ensures that all stakeholders have access to the foundational outcomes that drive all other domains of competency-based practices.

CHAPTER 3

Agency

There is a deep irony at the heart of traditional K–12 schooling: Students—for whom the entire educational enterprise exists—are often the least empowered members of a school community (Wenmoth et al., 2021). As Marzano and Kosena (2022) observed, "One might make the case that the traditional school structure is to some extent based on fostering conformity in students" (p. 163). Any endeavor to implement competency-based practices must flip this reality on its head.

Creating a supportive educational environment that values and fosters student agency offers numerous benefits related to academic, mental, and psychological fitness, including increased motivation, higher levels of engagement, and deeper learning. Psychologist Shane J. Lopez (2013) listed agency, along with goals and pathways, as a core competency of hopeful people. In this chapter, we discuss decisions schools need to make to ensure agency development is both explicit and embedded in their routines and procedures.

Before we define agency, let's distinguish between it and a closely related concept: efficacy. *Efficacy* refers to one's belief that one can do something. *Agency* refers to the actions one takes to do something (Marzano & Abbott, 2022; Marzano & Hardy, 2023). Table 3.1 (page 60) presents a selection of definitions of student agency; as illustrated in these definitions, agency and efficacy are often subsumed into a single conglomerate concept and labeled *agency*.

Table 3.1: Definitions of Student Agency

Source	Definition
Core Education, 2025	"Having the power, combined with choices, to take meaningful action and see the result of those decisions" (p. 12).
Education Policy Innovation Collaborative, 2021	"The choices that students can make about their own educational goals, learning, and the demonstration of that learning" (p. 13).
Jones, Avery, & DiMartino, 2020	"Students taking ownership of and responsibility for their own learning. . . . When students have a say in what and how they engage with content" (p. 14).
Nagaoka, Farrington, Ehrlich, & Heath, 2015	"The ability to make choices about and take an active role in one's life path, rather than being the product of one's circumstances" (p. 64).
Sutherland & Strunk, 2021	"Decisions made by students . . . to take ownership of their learning, shape their experiences, and become active agents in education instead of passive recipients" (p. 15).
Zima, 2021	"The perceived ability of the individual, based on his or her capacity, to shape his or her life" (p. 1).

Relative to student agency, there are two decisions that schools must make.

1. What programs and practices will we provide so that students experience a sense of agency?
2. What, if any, expected student outcomes will we establish for knowledge and skills regarding agency?

Many schools will likely decide to simply promote agency through programs and practices such as those described in this chapter. However, some schools may choose to explicitly articulate nonacademic outcomes related to student agency; be prepared that some of these outcomes may overlap with some of the cognitive, metacognitive, and self-system skills described in chapter 2 (page 39). This is perfectly acceptable, and we recommend consolidating similar outcomes into one measurement topic if this occurs. For example, agency-related measurement topics and student outcomes might include the following.

- **Self-regulated learning:** The student will demonstrate the ability to set goals, monitor their progress, and adjust strategies as needed.
- **Growth mindset development:** The student will show resilience when facing difficult tasks, use feedback to improve, and celebrate their progress.

- **Motivation and engagement:** The student will voluntarily explore topics beyond the curriculum and independently initiate discussions to deepen their understanding.
- **Goal setting and reflection:** The student will consistently set weekly learning goals and review them to identify strengths and areas for improvement.
- **Task management:** The student will manage their time and resources effectively without direct oversight.
- **Advocacy and voice:** The student will articulate their needs, ask questions, and seek help when necessary.

If a school decides to explicitly articulate agency-related measurement topics and outcomes, we strongly recommend that they craft proficiency scales for each, taking a grade-banded approach, as described in chapter 2 (page 39). Additionally, you will need to decide which structure and reporting approach (from the six scenarios described in chapter 1, page 25) you will use for agency-related measurement topics. In the pages that follow, we will consider different ways teachers can establish an agency-promoting environment, ensure student choice, co-create standard operating procedures, empower learners by designating jobs and roles for students, and prompt meaningful reflection.

Agency-Promoting Environment

Agency doesn't just happen; teachers must intentionally plan to develop agency in the classroom. Bill Zima (2021) suggested that learning experiences that encourage student agency have specific characteristics in common, such as the following.

- Well-defined learning goals
- An application of the knowledge gained in the unit
- Reflection before, during, and after learning
- A way to trigger wonder

The classroom context should allow for collaboration and the open sharing of ideas between the teacher and students and also between students and their peers. Teachers should design learning tasks with an intentional focus on developing students' agency; this increases the likelihood that students will develop the belief they can accomplish tasks because of the skills and knowledge they acquired during the task. Wenmoth and colleagues (2021) suggested using questions like those in table 3.2 to help educators think about the best ways to create a "partnership learning model" in classrooms (p. 15). The answer to these questions could lead a school or teacher to develop further programs and practices to reach the desired outcome of agency development.

Table 3.2: Questions for Creating a Partnership Learning Model

Purpose	Questions
Inviting Personal Initiative	• How will we teach students the right times and methods for taking personal initiative? • How will we design instructional activities and classroom procedures to encourage students to take individual initiative? • What reflective questions will help students engage in self-regulation when faced with challenges?
Cultivating Interdependence	• How can we create an interdependent ecosystem filled with opportunities for students to collaborate? • How will we recognize the role of individual students in contributing to their group's success?
Building a Productive Environment	• What systems and structures will best create and maintain a safe and organized learning environment? • How will we give students clear guidance (for example, posted norms, procedures, and other resources) about how to develop self-directed social and academic behaviors?

Source: Adapted from Wenmoth et al., 2021.

Overall, an agency-promoting environment is one that amplifies student voices. When students see that teachers are not just listening to their input but also acting on it, it lets them know that they have power. For example, teachers could do the following.

- Regularly hold classroom discussions encouraging students to share their thoughts
- Work with students to collaboratively set academic and behavior goals
- Create feedback loops where students can give feedback on lessons, activities, and even teaching approaches
- Hold student-led conferences, giving students the opportunity to lead the conversation about their progress, challenges, and goals
- Give students the opportunity to have input on the layout and setup of the classroom, choosing where to sit or rearranging furniture or supplies

- Allow students to take on teaching roles to promote leadership and collaboration
- Involve students in creating the classroom code of collaboration, rules, norms, and standard operating procedures

These types of activities can increase student engagement, build confidence in students, cause them to challenge ideas and think critically, prompt them to advocate for themselves and others, cultivate a sense of classroom community, teach students to respect differing viewpoints, and give them a taste of real-world decision making.

Student Choice

The heart of student choice involves building a culture of belonging and trust. When you ask students to participate in classroom decision-making processes, it communicates, "You are important to me, and your opinions matter." Research has shown that student choice works best within a balance of freedom and support; students don't seem interested in having an unlimited amount of choice in the classroom. Researchers Danielle Sutherland and Katharine O. Strunk (2021) drew the following conclusions on students' response to choice:

> *We find evidence to suggest that students have limited interest in making choices about content and how they will demonstrate what they've learned. For example, when asked if they wanted to direct their learning, many students expressed interest but said that they wanted to make these choices within a structure of support and guidance from their teachers. Other students expressed a strong desire to cede choice and control to their teachers. (p. 16)*

This is not due to immaturity. Research in adults has shown the inability to make a choice if too many options are provided; when people are presented with too many options, they can experience decision paralysis and dissatisfaction (Iyengar, 2023; Iyengar & Lepper, 2000; Schwartz, 2016). Thus, the goal when providing choice to students is to find an appropriate balance between freedom and support.

Wenmoth and colleagues (2021) suggested ways to maintain this balance using Wenmoth's (2013) domains of responsibility as an organizational structure, as shown in table 3.3 (page 64).

Table 3.3: Suggestions for Balancing Freedom and Support

Domain	Suggestions
Responsibility to Self	• Ensure that when you offer choice, you also provide frameworks and scaffolds so students can be intentional about the choices they make and the reasons for making them. • Provide opportunities for risk taking and for mistakes, but always ensure there is an opportunity to reflect on and learn from those mistakes. • Help students confront challenges when things get too difficult and provide encouragement and scaffolds for approaching problems. • Provide opportunities to learn about the consequences of making poor decisions, such as highlighting the impact of cyberbullying or ignoring others' advice.
Responsibility to Others	• When focusing on collaborative activity and group work, ensure the group has authentic ways to process choices and decisions. Assigning group roles can be a good starting point here, so over time groups will choose to assign roles themselves as they become more aware of individuals' strengths and contributions. • Take time to allow learners to process conflict in groups, learning to accept different points of view, express empathy, and work as part of a team. Provide assurance that this sort of thing is a natural part of how people address problems. Model these behaviors as teachers and use opportunities to explain this to students.
Responsibility to the Environment We Share	• In the immediate environment of the classroom or school, demonstrating this responsibility can include putting away library books, keeping the grounds litter free, cleaning the paint trays, disposing of waste materials or recycling materials, and making decisions about using natural products instead of plastics when selecting resources for school use. • For the broader environment of the community or world, examples include demonstrating concern for local or global environmental issues, such as the design and use of public spaces, pollution of local streams and waterways, treatment of refugees, and how local and national political decisions are made.

Source: Adapted from Wenmoth et al., 2021, pp. 14–15.

Marzano and Abbott (2022) offered a concrete example of enabling student choice within a well-structured learning task. If the class is learning to summarize content after reading, teachers can allow students to select the content that they want to read, using a website such as ReadWorks or CommonLit. Because the learning outcome is independent of the content in the text, teachers have a golden opportunity to offer an appropriate level of structured choice. For teachers, keeping the end goal in mind—the learning targets articulated in the proficiency scale—frees them to let students make many decisions on the way to that goal. For example, a teacher might pick any of the following prompts to give students choice.

- What kind of brain break should we do today?
- What book do we want to read next?
- What goal should we set as a class?
- What should be our reward for meeting the class goal?
- Which activity should we do first?
- What song should we listen to during work time today?
- What warm-up should we do tomorrow?
- How will you demonstrate your learning?
- Will you work by yourself, with a partner, or in a small group?
- What will your deadline be for this assignment?

Any time the teacher needs to make a choice—and there are many, many choices being made every day—they should ask themselves, "Is this a choice I am able to give to the students?" These small gifts of choice, repeated daily, can result in huge gains in student agency.

Finally, we recommend that teachers leverage the power of generative artificial intelligence (AI) to ease the preparation burden of offering students choice. For example, a teacher might poll students before a unit to find out what content is most interesting to them; if the learning goals for the unit are largely skill based (such as summarizing a text or analyzing arguments), students can practice them using a wide variety of content. Some students might be interested in Pokémon, others in the history of soccer, and others in a specific social media influencer. Generative AI can generate a host of materials focused on student-selected content, including project ideas, journal prompts, exit tickets, and brain breaks.

Additionally, for any textual needs, AI can write level-specific, skill-specific, and vocabulary-specific articles on almost any content desired. For example, if you want seven paragraphs about the history of music and social movements with a clear main idea and author opinions for your center rotations, generative AI can give it to you within seconds. We will add that it is also important to ask students to read texts written by human authors, but the creative possibilities of generative AI allow teachers to incorporate student interests and choice into instruction like never before (Burriss & Leander, 2024; Ciampa, Wolfe, & Bronstein, 2023; Daniel, Pacheco, Smith, Burriss, & Hundley, 2023; DeJulio et al., 2024; Hutchison, 2024; Kumar, Cotter, & Cabrera, 2024; Robinson & Hollet, 2024; Wagner, 2024).

Standard Operating Procedures

Possibly the best way to create a classroom balancing structure with freedom to promote student agency is by using standard operating procedures. According to Marzano and colleagues (2017), *standard operating procedures* are "sets of step-by-step instructions that support students in independently achieving desired results for routines and procedures on a consistent basis" (p. 49; see also Rao, Radhakrishnan, & Andrade, 2011, & Zima, 2021). Teachers and students can collaborate to create standard operating procedures for situations such as the following.

- Assignment submission
- Classroom discussion etiquette
- Classroom supply management
- Device usage
- End-of-day routines
- Entrance to the classroom
- Fire drills
- Lineup or movement between classes
- Lunch
- Permission to leave the classroom
- Recess
- Requests for help
- Restroom needs
- Transition between activities
- How to ask a peer or teacher for advice
- How to deliver a sincere apology
- How to log on to a computer
- How to maintain a good supply of commonly used materials (for example, pencils and markers)
- How to save your work while using technology
- How to set and reach a goal
- How to solve problems

- How to troubleshoot common computer issues
- How to work in small groups
- What to do if you finish your work early
- What to do when you are stuck
- What to do when you feel angry
- What to do when you make a mistake
- What to do when you're all done
- What to do if you were absent

Marzano and colleagues (2017) provided a process to use when creating standard operating procedures:

1. *Identify common inefficiencies that frequently require redirection, reminder, or more time than necessary.*
2. *Prioritize these based on need.*
3. *Determine the complexity and type of procedure. Does it require a procedural list or a flowchart?*
4. *Develop schoolwide and classroom procedures with student input. (p. 50)*

We strongly recommend that teachers collaborate with their class to develop a standard operating procedure anytime the teacher finds themselves answering the same question or managing the same situation repeatedly.

For example, if a teacher notices that students are taking too much time at the beginning of class to get settled, he might say, "I've noticed that we are just taking too much time at the beginning of class to get settled. I'd like your input on how we can get that fixed. First off, why might it be important for us to come in and get settled right away?" After students volunteer answers (to get started on work, to calm down after a break, to be quiet and listen to instruction) and the teacher records them on the board, he says, "I think it's important to understand the root cause. Why do you think students are taking so long to get settled in?" Students offer (and the teacher records) a variety of causes.

- Needing to get a drink
- Finishing up conversations from the hallway
- Seeing a friend and wanting to chat
- Needing to ask someone for a supply

The teacher winds up the discussion with two additional questions.

1. What steps do you think we can take to make sure we are able to do the things we need to do?
2. I want to value your needs as well. It sounds like some of the things that are happening are important to you. How can we ensure that your needs are being met?

As students list the steps and explain what they need, the teacher writes down their contributions. He concludes by telling them that he will use what they've shared to create a new standard operating procedure, which they will try out the next day.

It is important to remember that standard operating procedures aren't always perfect the first time they're drafted; they often need tweaks and adjustments that become apparent only once the class starts using them. Therefore, teachers should track the efficacy of standard operating procedures by answering the following questions with the class's input.

- Are we seeing the desired outcome?
- Are we reaching our goal?
- Do we need to adjust or revise anything?

Also, standard operating procedures should usually have a limited lifespan. Once a standard operating procedure has become a routine part of classroom procedure, it is appropriate to celebrate the class's success and then retire the obsolete standard operating procedure to make way for more pressing issues that need to be addressed.

Student Jobs and Roles

Wenmoth and colleagues (2021) found that implementing competency-based practices aimed at increasing student agency changed the roles and relationships between students and teachers in the classroom. They explained, "Roles and relationships will be different between student and teacher when agency is activated. Students will have more input into the classroom operations, creating a greater sense of equanimity between teacher and student over sharing of information and decision-making" (Wenmoth et al., 2021, p. 10).

You can speed up this process and encourage student agency by assigning students particular jobs and roles in the classroom. In fact, as Marzano and Abbott (2022) pointed out, many elementary classroom teachers already do this, assigning jobs such as line leaders, door holders, and so on. We strongly recommend that teachers at all levels take advantage of the efficiencies and student agency they can gain by allowing students to help with the small, routine jobs that often fill up teachers' days, leaving teachers free to spend time on tasks that only they can do. For example, at the primary level, potential student jobs include the following.

- Attendance assistant
- Calendar helper
- Cleanup captain
- Door holder
- Line leader
- Lunch monitor
- Messenger
- Quiet captain
- Supply supervisor
- Tech helper

Many of the primary teachers we've worked with will choose a daily "special helper." This student assumes many of the roles for a particular day. In some classrooms, the special helper is empowered to choose an assistant helper for the day, adding another element of student choice to the process. At the intermediate level, potential student jobs include the following.

- Class librarian
- Class photographer
- Classroom manager (oversees all classroom jobs)
- Discussion leader
- Homework checker
- Materials manager
- Peer tutor
- Point tracker
- Tech guru
- Timekeeper

For middle school and high school students, consider designing roles that emphasize and take advantage of students' strengths. For example, a student who is strong in grammar and spelling might be the class revision specialist. Someone with strengths in art might be the class illustrator and graphic design specialist. Other potential student jobs at the middle and high school levels include the following.

- Classroom manager
- Class scribe
- Event coordinator
- Homework monitor
- Librarian
- Materials coordinator
- Peer mentor
- Photographer
- Project manager
- Study group leader
- Tech support
- Timekeeper

If more structure is needed for student jobs and roles, consider creating a standard operating procedure for each classroom job. Jobs can also be rated and evaluated (or not), rewarded (or not), and rotated (or not). If more students want jobs than are available, ask them what types of jobs they think are needed. Overall, if you want students to feel ownership and agency over their school experience, allow them to be the ones who handle the routine tasks and activities that make the classroom work. We have heard from many teachers in competency-based classrooms that the most effective classes they have are the ones where they give up the most control. In the words of one teacher, "It's their class—let them run it."

Reflection

As noted previously, reflection is an important element of agency. Zima (2021) explained that "reflection is an activity that allows one to learn from decisions made and the impacts of those decisions. When humans reach goals by overcoming the obstacles on a chosen pathway, their perceived ability to shape their lives—agency—increases" (p. 100). While students can reflect at the end of the learning experience to see the knowledge and skills they have gained, Zima (2021) recommended that reflection occur during all learning stages.

- **Before learning**, students can reflect on their visualization of their end goal. Is it actually what they want to attain? Is it attainable in the time available? Is it attainable using the resources available? Students can begin to plan the actions needed to reach their goals.
- **During learning**, students can reflect on their progress as they monitor their pace and pathway toward the goal. Are their actions getting them closer to their goal? Are they getting there quickly enough? What obstacles have they encountered that they didn't expect, and what will they do to address those obstacles?
- **After learning**, students reflect on how it went. Did they reach their goal? If so, what is their next goal? If not, what will they do about that (for example, try again or change goals), and who can help them?

There are many strategies to incorporate reflection into class activities. Possibly the most flexible is the student journal, but teachers can also use exit tickets, self-assessment matrixes, and blogs or vlogs for reflection. Any medium or format that requires students to stop and ask themselves, "How is it going?" or "How did it go?" is appropriate. For example, before starting a unit about photosynthesis and respiration in science class, students state what they already know about these concepts and set a goal. During the unit, students use specific skills and knowledge from the proficiency scale to reflect on their progress and identify where they need additional support and who can provide this support. At the conclusion of the unit, students reflect on their progress compared to their goal and why they were or were not able to reach their goal.

As a more extended example, consider a teacher using a strategy called the Question Formulation Technique (Right Question Institute, 2024). To use the Question Formulation Technique, the teacher provides students with a prompt and allows them to generate questions. For example, for the topic of human body systems, the teacher might provide the prompt, "How do the different human body systems work together to maintain homeostasis?" The questions can be anything related to the prompt. For example, students might generate the following questions.

- How does the circulatory system interact with the respiratory system?
- What is the role of the nervous system in regulating body functions?
- How do the digestive and excretory systems collaborate to remove waste from the body?
- What systems are involved in fighting infections?

- How do the endocrine and reproductive systems work together?
- How do muscles and bones coordinate to allow movement?
- What is homeostasis, and why is it important for human survival?
- What happens if one body system stops functioning properly?
- How does the cardiovascular system maintain blood pressure?
- How do different body systems adapt to stress?

The students then choose their three favorite questions, refine them, prioritize them, and research answers to them. For example:

1. In what ways do the circulatory and respiratory systems work together to oxygenate the body?
2. How do the immune, circulatory, and lymphatic systems collaborate to fight infections?
3. What role do the nervous and endocrine systems play in maintaining homeostasis in the human body?

To incorporate reflection into the activity, the teacher could use prompts before students begin research.

- **What do I already know about the human body systems, and how can that help me focus my research?** This question encourages students to think about their prior knowledge, such as names of systems they've heard before (for example, circulatory and respiratory systems), and identify gaps they want to explore.

- **What do I need to learn to better understand how these systems work together?** Students reflect on the overarching goal of understanding how body systems interact. This helps them shape questions that explore relationships between systems, not just individual functions. It begins to help them set action steps to help them reach the learning goal of the task.

- **How can my questions guide me toward the learning goal of understanding how body systems work together?** By reflecting on how their questions will support their learning goal, students ensure that they generate meaningful questions. For example, they focus on questions like "How does the digestive system support the circulatory system?" instead of only simple factual ones.

As students engage in research, the teacher can use additional reflection prompts.

- **Are the answers I'm finding helping me understand how body systems work together?** This question prompts students to evaluate whether their research is meaningful. For example, if they are learning facts only about individual systems (such as "The heart pumps blood"), they can adjust to ask how the circulatory system supports other systems.

- **Do I need to revise or expand my questions to better understand how these systems interact?** Students reflect on whether their original questions need adjustment. If a group finds that learning about the nervous system opens new questions such as "How does the brain communicate with muscles to help us move?" they can adjust their focus to ensure their research is thorough.

- **Am I finding information that directly connects to the learning goal?** Answering this question helps students assess whether they are finding relevant data. For instance, if they spend too much time on the anatomy of the heart, the reflection question helps them refocus on discovering how the circulatory system interacts with other systems.

At the end of their research, the teacher prompts students to reflect on their understanding and determine whether they've met the learning goals.

- **Did my research help me understand how the body systems work together?** This reflection question encourages students to compare their findings to the original learning goal. If they realize they've focused on only one system, they might need to revisit their research and expand their exploration of other systems.

- **What evidence do I have that explains the connection between body systems?** This question prompts students to reflect on specific examples they've learned. They might explain how the respiratory system provides oxygen to the circulatory system, which transports it to the body's cells.

- **Are there any questions I still have about body systems or areas where I need more understanding?** Students reflect on any lingering questions or uncertainties. This helps them identify areas for further learning, such as the role of the endocrine system in regulating bodily functions.

- **How does my understanding of body systems connect to real-life situations, like exercise or illness?** This helps students apply their knowledge to practical situations, making the learning more meaningful. For example, they could reflect on how exercise increases the need for oxygen, which highlights the relationship between the respiratory and circulatory systems.

These reflection prompts guide students' inquiry and ensure they are thinking critically about how human body systems interact and support each other.

Summary

Fostering student agency goes beyond simply encouraging students to take ownership of their learning. Agency is cultivated through structured opportunities for initiative, reflection, and real-world applications of knowledge. Setting clear goals, leveraging student voice through student-led discussions, integrating student choice into daily decisions and personalized learning tools, and designing standard operating procedures empower students to make productive decisions during their learning journeys. All these strategies shift the power dynamics of the classroom away from the teacher and toward the students, creating a learning environment that fosters self-advocacy and equity, topics which we discuss in the next chapter.

CHAPTER 4

Equity

In many ways, implementing competency-based practices is synonymous with implementing more equitable practices. Ruyle and colleagues (2025) asserted that true equity, cultural affirmation, and inclusion can be fully realized only in schools where mastery-based learning principles are effectively implemented. In such a setting, equity entails articulating high expectations for every learner and creating concrete plans to achieve those expectations while also embracing diversity, respecting individual identities, and valuing cultural heritage.

Creating a system that moves away from standardization and instead seeks to identify and support the specific needs of students aligns with many of the definitions of equity. Table 4.1 presents a selection of those definitions.

Table 4.1: Definitions of Equity

Source	Definition of Equity
Glossary of Education Reform (2016)	"[Equity] refers to the principle of fairness. While it is often used interchangeably with the related principle of *equality*, equity encompasses a wide variety of educational models, programs, and strategies that may be considered fair, but not necessarily equal. It is has been said that 'equity is the process; equality is the outcome,' given that equity—what is fair and just—may not, in the process of educating students, reflect strict equality—what is applied, allocated, or distributed equally."

continued →

Source	Definition of Equity
Great Schools Partnership (2024)	"Ensuring just outcomes for each student, raising marginalized voices, and challenging the imbalance of power and privilege."
National Equity Project (n.d.)	"Each child receives what they need to develop to their full academic and social potential. Working toward equity in schools involves: • Ensuring equally high outcomes for all participants in our educational system; removing the predictability of success or failures that currently correlates with any social or cultural factor; • Interrupting inequitable practices, examining biases, and creating inclusive multicultural school environments for adults and children; and • Discovering and cultivating the unique gifts, talents, and interests that every human possesses."
Noguera, Darling-Hammond, & Friedlaender (2015)	"Policies and practices that ensure that every student has access to an education focused on *meaningful learning* (i.e., that teaches the deeper learning skills contemporary society requires in ways that empower students to learn independently), taught by competent and caring educators who are able to attend to the student's social and academic needs, and supported by *adequate resources* that provide the materials and conditions for effective learning" (p. 3).
OECD (2012)	"Equity in education means that personal or social circumstances such as gender, ethnic origin or family background, are not obstacles to achieving educational potential (fairness) and that all individuals reach at least a basic minimum level of skills (inclusion)" (p. 37).
Thompson & Thompson (2018)	"An equitable system . . . does not treat all students in a standardized way, but differentiates instruction, services, and resources to respond effectively to students' diverse needs so that each student can develop his or her full academic and societal potential" (p. 36).

Those who advocate for the use of competency-based practices to promote equity argue that the purpose of the U.S. education system has changed since the early 20th century, and, therefore, the structure of that system also needs to change. Specifically, Carla M. Evans, Suzanne E. Graham, and Melissa L. Lefebvre (2019) explained the following:

> The underlying premise is that the U.S. education system perpetuates educational inequities and lackluster quality because it follows an outdated traditional model of education that was designed in the early 20th century to rank and sort large numbers of students into college preparatory or career and technical classes. . . .

> *In comparison, a competency-based model of education has its foundations in the progressive education movement with the expectation that school should be child-centered. . . . CBE is rooted in the belief that all students can learn the material if given the time and opportunity to demonstrate mastery in order to move on in the curriculum and eventually graduate with the necessary knowledge, skills, and dispositions. (p. 301)*

When teachers have the resources and pedagogical expertise to ensure all students are proficient in the expected learning outcomes and able to meet high expectations regardless of socioeconomic status or cultural background, mastery-based principles can empower all learners to reach their full potential. This approach prioritizes learning outcomes over the specific materials used, allowing for the incorporation of culturally relevant and engaging instructional materials. By using resources and perspectives that resonate with students' backgrounds and interests, we create a more inclusive and accessible learning environment. This helps students connect more deeply with the content, enhancing both engagement and comprehension while avoiding reliance on unfamiliar material. This can, ultimately, promote a more equitable and inclusive society.

Similar to agency, there are two decisions that schools must make relative to equity.

1. What programs and practices will we provide so that students experience a sense of equity and inclusion?
2. What, if any, expected student outcomes will we establish for knowledge and skills regarding equity and inclusion?

In this chapter, we articulate several programs and practices that you could use to promote equity and inclusion. You may also choose to explicitly articulate student outcomes related to equity and inclusion, such as the following.

- **Cultural awareness and competency:** The student will demonstrate understanding of and respect for diverse cultures, perspectives, and identities.

- **Antibias attitudes and inclusive language:** The student will actively use inclusive language and reject bias, stereotypes, and discrimination.

- **Empathy and perspective taking:** The student will understand and consider the experiences and viewpoints of others, especially those different from their own.

- **Awareness of social justice issues:** The student will demonstrate understanding of social justice topics and think critically about equity, fairness, and systemic issues.

- **Allyship and advocacy:** The student will support and stand up for others who might be experiencing bias, exclusion, or discrimination.
- **Conflict resolution and dialogue:** The student will engage respectfully in conversations about differences, addressing conflicts thoughtfully and without escalation.
- **Cross-cultural communication:** The student will communicate effectively across cultural and language differences.

If you choose to explicitly articulate outcomes related to equity and inclusion, these may or may not overlap with the cognitive, metacognitive, and self-system skills described in chapter 2 (page 39). Regardless of any overlap, it is helpful to keep in mind that some of these outcomes may be similar in nature to metacognitive and self-system skills in that their use (and therefore their assessment) is situational. Proficiency scales for these outcomes will likely need to include targets that involve a student monitoring their levels of the equity or inclusion skill while engaged in social or learning interactions. As a reminder, if you choose to articulate equity- and inclusion-related outcomes, you will need to decide which structure and reporting scenario (of the six described in chapter 1, page 25) you will use for those outcomes.

In the following pages, we focus on teacher decision making as it relates to addressing power dynamics, systemic injustice, and the reality of inequitable teacher quality.

Power Dynamics

Many of the concepts associated with equity and inclusion are related to the agency concepts discussed in chapter 3 (page 59). For example, according to researchers Liliana M. Garces and Cynthia Gordon da Cruz (2017), power is closely related to agency. As Garces and Gordon da Cruz (2017) defined the term, *power* means "having the capacity to do something, such as to carry out one's wishes or to access resources and opportunities that impact one's life" (p. 331). Relative to equity, educator Anne-Marie Núñez (2014; see also Núñez, Rivera, & Hallmark, 2020) highlighted four domains in which power and privilege must be examined and imbalances addressed.

1. **Organizational power:** The positions people hold in societal structures such as work, family, and education can give those people more or less power.

2. **Representational power:** The ways in which groups of people are portrayed in the media, in everyday conversation, and in cultural imagery can give groups of people more or less power.

3. **Intersubjective power:** The relationships between individuals and between groups of people can give the people in those groups more or less power.

4. **Experiential power:** The ways in which people make sense of their experiences and tell stories about their lives can increase or decrease their power.

One of the central power dynamics in schools is between students and the teacher. Traditionally, teachers have wielded power and students have not. But competency-based practices recommend changing that power dynamic. One way to do this is by creating standard operating procedures for discussions, especially discussions around issues of race, politics, and inequalities. Educators Jordan A. Arellanes and Michael Hendricks (2022) recommended creating guidelines for class discussions that incorporate "a method whereby the instructor and students alike could hold each other accountable if any questionable statements were made in class. An equal way of holding each other accountable demonstrates that all voices are equally valued" (p. 372).

Another power dynamic in schools occurs between individuals from different cultures. It is important to keep in mind that culture does not necessarily align with race; racially similar students and teachers might have significant cultural differences, depending on their backgrounds, family histories, and experiences. To address power imbalances stemming from cultural differences, educators and students can practice cultural humility.

Cultural humility, according to educator Don E. Davis and colleagues (2018), as well as researchers Marcie Fisher-Borne, Jessie Montana Cain, and Suzanne L. Martin (2015), involves acknowledging and examining one's own and others' cultural identities with the goal of eliminating power imbalances. Psychologists Dena M. Abbott, Noelany Pelc, and Caitlin Mercier (2019) provided the following seven recommendations for those in educational settings seeking to develop cultural humility.

1. **Self-reflection:** Engage in ongoing self-reflection to evaluate your cultural identity, including privilege and marginalization, and how this impacts your interactions with others.

2. **Lifelong learning:** Commit to lifelong cultural learning to remain aware of contemporary issues and facilitate difficult dialogues with respect to others' lived experiences.

3. **Salient identities:** Allow others to determine which identities are salient to them, creating space for them to define themselves and share their experiences.

4. **Developmental approach:** Intentionally cultivate environments where cultural humility can thrive, encouraging a developmental approach to understanding culture and fostering open dialogue and acceptance.

5. **Learning materials:** Develop course content and assignments that foster cultural humility among students, incorporating activities and materials that encourage critical consciousness and understanding of diverse perspectives.

6. **Mentorship:** Provide mentorship experiences that honor students' cultural identities and facilitate open discussions about cultural differences, recognizing the impact of systemic power imbalances and advocating for their mentees.

7. **Awareness of limitations:** Demonstrate awareness of the limitations of traditional teaching methods and be open to incorporating alternative approaches that are more inclusive and representative of diverse experiences, promoting culturally humble practices.

In addition to the power dynamics involved in student-teacher interactions and those stemming from cultural differences, there is a power dynamic in schools between instructional materials and methods and students of diverse backgrounds. According to researchers Wendy Surr, Kim Carter, and Andrea Stewart (2022), "Teachers must be culturally responsive when introducing new concepts, finding ways to link new ideas with students' personal and cultural experiences and cognitive frames" (p. 12). One way to address this power imbalance is through a lesson study approach to designing instruction that incorporates student voices and preferences, especially the voices and preferences of students from minority ethnic backgrounds.

Educator Mel Ainscow (2020) described how three teachers engaged in this approach preparing a joint lesson. After first identifying "particularly vulnerable" students in their classes, including one who elected not to speak even when prompted and another with dyslexia, they began to brainstorm:

> *New and different ways of facilitating the learning of all of their students. . . .*
> *They talked, for example, about getting the students to write on the whiteboard,*

> *and getting students to rehearse verbally what they wanted to say, rather than writing arguments down.*
>
> *The trio decided that they needed to involve some of their students before teaching the lesson to get an idea of how they preferred to learn. They also wanted to consider how best to plan the lesson to support the many differences amongst the students. They therefore selected seven students, each from a different ethnic background, six of whom were born outside the country. The teachers got these students together at lunchtime and asked them to rank their preferences regarding different classroom activities that might be used when studying poetry. (Ainscow, 2020, pp. 10–11)*

Marzano and Abbott (2022) suggested the following activities that teachers might also use to give their students power and voice relative to classroom functioning:

- **Daily data collection:** *A routine activity where students submit data to the teacher regarding their status or growth on the proficiency scales for specific measurement topics*
- **Weekly conferences:** *A routine conference between teacher and students to discuss academic topics and bring up any issues and concerns*
- **Parking lot:** *A piece of chart paper or section of whiteboard where students can leave comments about how the class functions, often divided into sections for positive comments, questions, ideas, and things that need to change*
- **Peaks and valleys:** *A feedback opportunity, perhaps during daily or weekly wrap-up meetings, where students share their highs and lows from a certain time period or experience* (p. 131)

In summary, addressing power dynamics in the classroom requires intentional strategies that promote equity and amplify student voice. Educators can reshape traditional hierarchies by establishing accountable and inclusive discussion protocols, practicing cultural humility, and designing culturally responsive lessons. By involving students in instructional planning and feedback processes, teachers can create a more empowering and inclusive learning environment that values and respects diverse perspectives.

Systemic Injustice

In many cases, injustice and inequity are preserved because of what the majority groups think of as "normal." Educators Angela Calabrese Barton and Edna Tan (2020) said, "Systemic injustices are made invisible through their regularities in practice" (p. 433). It is important to note that adults in the school community set the tone for how equity is practiced. If they are not actively addressing issues of inequity and systemic injustice (which are often embedded in regular practices), efforts to include all students may remain superficial or inconsistent.

In this way, addressing equity goes beyond curriculum adjustments and student interactions; it involves educators continuously reflecting on their own biases, learning about the cultural contexts of their students, and adjusting their teaching practices accordingly. Schools must integrate this ongoing professional learning into their culture, ensuring that every educator is committed to deeply understanding the cultural dynamics that affect student learning. One strategy for encouraging this type of learning and addressing systemic injustice is disrupting the regularities of classroom practice.

Researchers Melissa L. Morgan Consoli and Patricia Marin (2016) suggested that educators can begin this process by communicating to students that the classroom is a space where open expression of ideas is valued and differing opinions can be held and examined without discounting or devaluing those who share them. For example, during the first few days of school with a new class, teachers not only introduce students to the content they will be learning but also set aside time for students to share about their backgrounds. According to psychologist Celia Jaes Falicov (2014), you should also share about your background, including how you came to know the content you will be teaching students, as well as the lenses through which you view that content.

You should also invite students to discuss ways in which they can or cannot relate to the topics they're learning, how they see their roles in the class, and how they think you can best support their needs (Arellanes & Hendricks, 2022). Relative to specific disciplines and content areas, invite students to engage in rightful presence activities. Calabrese Barton and Tan (2020) described *rightful presence* as challenging "what has been considered legitimate, possible and desirable within disciplinary learning" (p. 438). Rightful presence activities help students reshape the norms of a discipline to match their identities rather than shaping their identities to the norms of the discipline. According to Calabrese Barton and Tan (2020), this concept "asserts that legitimately belonging in a place . . . [involves] *making present* the political struggles guests embody and experience" (p. 434). Moreover, when teachers facilitate these opportunities for students to rethink their roles within and connections to the learning environment, they are "fostering new possibilities for future-oriented identity development" (Calabrese Barton & Tan, 2020, p. 436).

For instance, in a science classroom, you might ask students to explore how scientific concepts relate to their own communities or personal experiences. You could begin by having students investigate a local environmental issue, such as water quality, air pollution, or access to green spaces. This approach allows students to bring their unique backgrounds and perspectives into the study of science, making the content more relevant and fostering rightful presence by showing that their identities and experiences are valuable within the discipline. Through this, students start to see themselves as legitimate contributors to scientific conversations and feel more empowered to challenge or expand traditional understandings of science in ways that reflect their communities' needs and values.

Inequitable Teacher Quality

Teacher quality is an equity issue. Researchers Doris L. Thompson and Sherwood Thompson (2018) reported on two studies that found that low-income and minority students were more frequently taught by the least qualified teachers. To address this, a school implementing competency-based practices must emphasize teacher development. The first step in addressing teacher development is to adopt a model of instruction. As Marzano and Kosena (2022) explained, "A school's instructional model should be written in a detailed document and formally adopted by the school, creating a common language for educators to reference during self-assessment, professional development, goal setting, observations, and feedback" (p. 50).

As a school develops its instructional model, teachers can create demonstration classrooms to exemplify various aspects of the instructional model. Marzano and Hardy (2023) defined a *demonstration classroom* as "one that other teachers and interested members of various constituent groups can visit to observe the implementation of various components of the model the school is creating" (p. 17). Once the instructional model is in place, teachers should complete a self-reflection survey, assigning a score to themselves for each element of the model. As Marzano and Kosena (2022) observed, this exercise is not just to provide self-rating scores for administrators (although that is a productive purpose):

> Most often, high-quality instructional models are too complex to go over in a staff meeting, or even break down over several meetings. When each teacher is expected to digest every scale for self-assessment, the learning model itself is clearly communicated with tangible evidence provided. . . . This communication tactic is especially important for those elements in the model that are not commonly found in traditional instructional models, such as metacognitive skills or the development of student agency. Using teacher self-evaluation as a communication tool helps the principal clearly define the exact expectations teachers will be held to. (pp. 53–54)

Teacher self-assessment ratings then form the basis each teacher uses to set professional growth goals. These goals should focus on areas of the instructional model for which the teacher rated themselves at a beginning or developing level. Marzano and colleagues (2021) recommended that teachers set three professional growth goals per year.

Once a high-quality instructional model is in place and teachers have internalized the model by setting professional growth goals, the school or district can use teacher growth goal data to provide job-embedded professional development matched to the needs of each teacher. One of the more powerful methods for professional learning in any school is a practice called *instructional rounds*. According to Marzano and Kosena (2022), instructional rounds "involves a small group of teachers, guided by a leader or instructional coach, observing another teacher's lesson for the purpose of learning from that teacher's instructional practice" (p. 60). After the observation, the leader or instructional coach facilitates a discussion about what participants saw in the observed classroom.

Ideally, instructional rounds groups will be organized around participating teachers' growth goals. So, for example, if four teachers in a building had professional growth goals about previewing upcoming content, the leader or instructional coach could schedule an observation with them in the classroom of a teacher who was exceptionally good at previewing new content. In addition to benefiting the professional growth of individual teachers, instructional rounds—when implemented as a schoolwide practice—also support the development of a healthy collaborative team environment. Marzano and Kosena (2022) further explained the benefits of instructional rounds as follows:

> *Instructional rounds enhance the professional culture of a school, helping to break down the traditional teaching silos that exist in many schools by providing opportunities for teachers to observe their colleagues and discuss instructional practice.*
>
> *Guided instructional rounds also leverage the strengths of existing faculty to improve the overall instructional capacity of the building. Since teachers only observe other teachers in only those areas they are strong in, guided instructional rounds provide opportunities for individual teachers' strengths to be highlighted. Guided instructional rounds are a win-win for a school and are highly recommended as part of any professional development model. (p. 60)*

Sutherland and Strunk (2021) reported on Lehigh Public Schools in Michigan, a district that implemented instructional rounds practices, which they called *classroom learning labs*. Sutherland and Strunk (2021) described Lehigh's experience:

> *Lehigh created classroom learning labs, which created opportunities for teachers to observe peers for targeted instructional demonstrations. . . . Teachers collaborate in multi-grade cohorts and develop common professional development goals that inform their learning labs. . . . Lehigh [instructional] coaches help to plan and facilitate the learning labs. For example, in 2019–2020, one cohort focused on individualized pacing and small group instruction, while another focused on social-emotional learning. Creating shared learning goals and targeting observations to these goals make the learning labs more valuable to teachers. As part of these labs, teachers participate in pre- and post-observation collaboration and reflection. While many professional developments offer high-leverage practices, the pre- and post-conference discussion and reflective components add the opportunity for teachers to work with colleagues and receive support in adapting these new practices for their classrooms. (p. 8)*

While various leaders in a school can lead instructional rounds, the rounds are a particularly effective way for school administrators to productively share in professional learning conversations. For example, in Westminster Public Schools (where they call instructional rounds *learning walks*), school and district leaders regularly participate in instructional rounds at various schools each month (Gotto et al., 2025). Their inclusion in these professional learning teams deepens their knowledge of the instructional practices used throughout each school and helps them develop the language needed to provide quality feedback to support teacher growth.

Summary

Equity must be embedded both in teaching practices and in the power dynamics in schools. Respecting students' diverse values and backgrounds enables teachers to better support all learners, address systemic barriers, and create environments that value individual identities and needs. Additionally, ongoing professional growth and learning for educators are critical elements of ensuring equity by implementing competency-based practices.

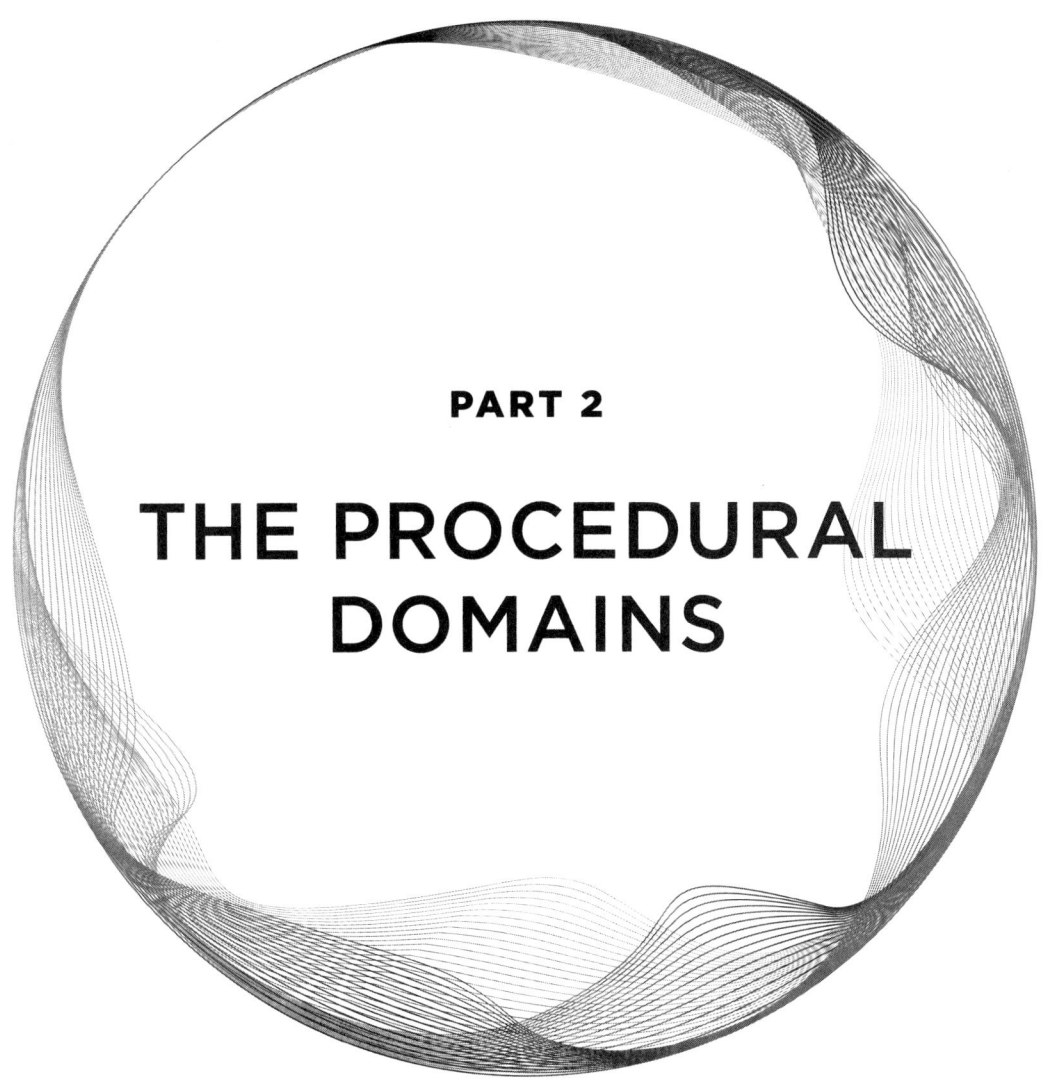

PART 2

THE PROCEDURAL DOMAINS

The three procedural domains—(1) assessment, (2) instruction, and (3) adult roles—focus on the key processes involved in the regular functioning of competency-based practices. To effectively measure student learning, you must choose appropriate assessments and determine how to calculate summative scores. To provide effective instruction, you must decide how to plan, how to introduce and reinforce content, and how to align resources to learning targets. To ensure that schools function effectively, you must clarify the roles and responsibilities of the adults in the system. Together, the procedural domains comprise the decisions and choices that bring your implementation of competency-based practices to life.

CHAPTER 5

Assessment

An *assessment* is any event that gathers and provides information about a student's knowledge and skill. It is during assessment that students and teachers attempt to make plain the otherwise invisible process of thinking. Assessment may involve formal questions administered on paper or computer, but it might also be a passing comment or something the teacher sees over a student's shoulder. Marzano, Aschoff, and Avila (2022) described the deciding factor that makes something an assessment: "When students implicitly or explicitly exhibit any type of evidence of their knowledge and skills, such evidence qualifies as an assessment if the teacher can assign a score to it" (p. 40). This broadly expanded definition of assessment is the bedrock on which a competency-based system of assessment is built.

In this book, we intentionally address assessment before instruction because, in a system implementing competency-based practices, instruction is driven by determinations of competence. As Evans and colleagues (2020) stated, "Determining competence is fundamentally an assessment decision" (p. 1). As they elaborated, "the factors that most strongly facilitate CBE implementation are those that provide teachers and students with clear procedures and tools to *identify the status of students along a learning progression*" (p. 22, emphasis added). Similarly, reporting on behalf of the Aurora Institute and the Center for Assessment, Scott Marion, Maria Worthen, and Carla Evans (2020) said the following:

> The determination of mastery must be based on assessment, broadly speaking. Furthermore, the determination of whether a student should move on or not

> *may be a fairly consequential decision, which has important implications for the quality of the assessment or assessments and for how assessment results are considered among multiple measures of student learning. (p. 8)*

Failing to prioritize the construction of a highly effective assessment system is a common mistake in schools seeking to implement competency-based practices. Evans and colleagues (2020) hypothesized that this is because "schools and teachers do not see assessment as part of the initial wave of implementing CB practices" (p. 21). This is a fatal error. Without a comprehensive and accurate assessment system, there is no way to identify the status (or pace) of students. In sum, a system of competency-based practices is only as good as the assessment system that drives it.

Make no mistake—constructing a highly effective assessment system is a challenging process. Assessment systems in schools implementing competency-based practices must serve several purposes. First, they must provide timely and detailed data to facilitate instructional feedback and track student progress on individual measurement topics. Second, assessments should be learner centered, providing opportunities for students to take ownership of their learning through voice and choice. This ensures that assessments not only track progress but also engage students in meaningful ways, further supporting their individual learning paths. Third, they must align with state assessments to ensure that students who demonstrate proficiency in the classroom are more likely to demonstrate proficiency on large-scale assessments. Fourth, they need to support and feed into the admissions processes of colleges and universities; students should not be penalized at the postsecondary level for attending a competency-based secondary school. As researchers Andrea J. Bingham, Matthew Adams, and Randall Lee Stewart (2021) stated eloquently, "CBE programs have to align with state standards to ensure adequate performance on state assessments . . . while also developing a system to communicate with and align to higher education's more traditional systems of learning" (p. 677).

Four questions guide a school's decision making on assessment.

1. How will our assessment system combine and align results from classroom, interim, and year-end assessments?
2. How will we ensure validity, reliability, and unidimensionality in classroom assessments?
3. What types of assessments will we use to measure outcomes?
4. How will we determine summative scores for students?

In this chapter, we discuss options for answering each of these questions and recommend specific approaches that align with best practices in educational assessment and measurement. We begin with a closer look at assessment systems and classroom assessment design before exploring scoring and grading and the significance of data notebooks.

Assessment Systems

The educational measurement literature we survey in this section provides guidance about the design of effective assessment systems. Specifically, effective assessment systems do the following.

- Accurately measure both academic and nonacademic knowledge and skills (Marzano et al., 2017)
- Base judgments on individual performance rather than comparing students to other students (as when grading on a curve; Gervais, 2016)
- Clearly articulate learning targets, including foundational and more complex content related to each learning target (Camacho & Legare, 2016; Marzano et al., 2017)
- Clearly explain the connection between assessment activities and the knowledge and skills being measured (Camacho & Legare, 2016)
- Correlate assessment scores across classroom assessments, benchmark or interim assessments, and large-scale assessments to ensure alignment and predictability of student performance (Camacho & Legare, 2016)
- Ensure accurate reporting of specific knowledge and skills and comparability of scores across assessments (Camacho & Legare, 2016; Marzano et al., 2017)
- Judge student learning in ways that are compatible with how student learning typically progresses, such as using growth curves instead of averages (Marion et al., 2020)
- Provide multiple opportunities and methods for students to demonstrate knowledge and skill (Marion et al., 2020)
- Record assessment data for ease of sharing with multiple audiences, including teachers, students, and parents (Gervais, 2016; Marzano et al., 2017)
- Use assessments intentionally as needed and for multiple purposes (Gervais, 2016; Marion et al., 2020; Marzano et al., 2017)
- Use assessments that access both student behaviors and student thought processes (Camacho & Legare, 2016)

- Use patterns of assessment data over time to inform all stakeholders about a student's specific learning needs to focus instruction most effectively (Gervais, 2016; Marion et al., 2020; Marzano et al., 2017)

Marzano and colleagues (2019) recommended creating a system of assessments that layers data from different types of assessments to create a complete picture of student status and growth. Figure 5.1 illustrates a general model for such an assessment system.

Classroom Assessments	☐☐☐☐☐☐☐☐☐ ↓↓↓↓↓↓↓↓↓	Standards
Interim Assessments	☐☐☐☐ ↓↓↓↓	
Year-End Assessments	☐	

Source: Marzano, 2018, p. 6.
Figure 5.1: Comprehensive competency-based assessment system.

Think of the levels of the assessment system in figure 5.1 in terms of specificity. Regarding assessment systems, Marzano and colleagues (2019) said the following:

> *One way to think about the three types of assessments that comprise the assessment system is to consider them in terms of the level of information they provide, moving from individual students (classroom) to classrooms (interim) to schools and districts (year-end or state). (p. 105)*

The critical point of contact in a competency-based assessment system is the classroom assessment because it gives the most granular level of detail about individual student status and growth. As Marzano and Kosena (2022) stated:

> *The main source of data about student learning is classroom assessments. . . . They provide daily and ongoing evidence of students' status and growth. Given that classroom assessments are designed around measurement topics and proficiency scales, they assess students' knowledge at a very granular level of detail. (p. 126)*

Classroom assessments are directly tied to what is taught in the classroom and are adjustable to meet individual learners' needs, including their interests, passions, and previous learning. Feedback obtained from classroom assessments can be delivered more quickly, including the possibility of in-the-moment feedback. Using this readily available feedback, teachers can also adjust the assessment context midstream to challenge a student more deeply or to align better with the student's cultural context, interests, and needs. In some cases, an assessment activity for determining the current status of one learning target can be augmented on the fly to include a preassessment for the next learning target. As discussed previously, classroom assessments can also detect the presence or absence of situational skills, such as metacognitive, self-system, agency, and equity outcomes.

The middle level of a competency-based assessment system is *interim* (also called *benchmark*) *assessments*. Interim assessments are "typically designed and administered by organizations outside of the school or school system (that is, testing companies) and are used to gauge student growth but not at the level of granularity of classroom assessments" (Marzano & Kosena, 2022, p. 126). One example is the NWEA Measures of Academic Progress, but there are many others that schools and districts can use. Interim assessments should reinforce and confirm the evidence of the classroom assessments, but it is important to remember that—although they may purport otherwise—they almost always provide data that are most useful and applicable at the classroom level rather than the individual student level. Teachers can use data from interim assessments to course correct their practices once or twice a year, compared to the daily and weekly adjustments that classroom assessments facilitate. Marzano and Kosena (2022) explained, "The progress monitoring that occurs during the [interim] assessment window provides timely information that teachers can use to make midyear corrections" (p. 115). Remember that while interim assessments can provide some broadly useful data about individual student status and growth, they are simply not administered frequently enough, nor do they contain enough assessment items, to achieve the level of specificity, immediacy, and instructionally useful insight that classroom assessments yield.

A successful competency-based assessment system functions against and aligns with the backdrop of *year-end assessments* (also called *state assessments* or *state tests*). State assessments have been widely criticized for being inequitable and culturally biased. Research has shown that these tests often fail to account for the diverse backgrounds of students, placing minority and low-income students at a disadvantage. As a result, according to pedagogical theorist Gloria Ladson-Billings (2014), these tests may not accurately reflect the abilities of students from different cultural or socioeconomic groups. But despite their limitations, state assessments remain the primary tool used by states to measure school and district performance. Data from these tests can confirm or disaffirm data collected through classroom and interim assessments but usually arrive too late for educators to take immediate corrective action to address issues highlighted in the data. Data from year-end tests are best used to ensure that systems of classroom and interim assessments align with state standards and state requirements for demonstrating proficiency.

Ideally, students who perform well on classroom assessments and interim assessments will also perform well on state assessments. If they don't, classroom assessment systems and interim assessment systems (and likely instructional systems) will need adjustment. As Marzano and colleagues (2019) stated, "If we are to assess students in the most accurate and useful ways, then we must think in terms of merging the information from classroom assessments with other types of assessments" (p. 1). Many refer to such an assessment system as a *balanced assessment system*. The National Research Council (2001) described balanced assessment systems as those that "comprehensively provide multiple sources of evidence to support educational decision-making, and they continuously document student progress over time" (p. 4). These kinds of balanced assessment systems are built, not born and, so far, are somewhat rare in K–12 education. In fact, Marion and colleagues (2020) said that "balanced assessment systems have been called the unicorns of educational assessment because they are rarely seen in the wild" (p. 9). Given that such a system of competency-based assessment is founded on a well-designed system of classroom assessment, we provide a high level of detail about building a strong system of classroom assessment here.

Classroom Assessment Design

Competency-based practices center on a single idea—flexibility to meet students' needs—and competency-based classroom assessments are no exception. Evans and colleagues (2019) listed the following ways in which competency-based classroom assessments must be flexible:

- *Administration of assessments (e.g., when assessments are administered to students)*
- *Opportunity for students to reassess*
- *Use of multiple measures*
- *Types of assessments used to determine student mastery or proficiency (p. 323)*

Researchers Heather M. Buzick, Jodi M. Casabianca, and Melissa L. Gholson (2023) offered a continuum of assessment approaches ranging from less to more flexible. As opposed to the same assessment experience for all, they noted that more flexible approaches offer test takers the following.

- Access to different tools (magnifying glass, calculator, and so forth)
- Selection of item prompts or possibly item formats

- Multiple item choices targeted toward more personal characteristics
- Options for form of provided evidence

As you design a flexible system of classroom assessments, you must remember the critical principle at the heart of all assessment practices: All assessments contain error (Marzano, 2018; Marzano et al., 2017; Simms, 2024). There is no perfect, definitive assessment because that's not how assessment works. Professional psychometricians constantly emphasize this point because it is so basic to the entire assessment endeavor. For example, Kathleen M. Sheehan (2017) of the Educational Testing Service wrote, "All assessment involves reasoning under uncertainty; we observe what students have said or done in a few specific instances, and then use that evidence to support inferences about what students know and can do more generally" (p. 36).

In other words, assessment is at least as much art as science. When designing classroom assessments, the art and science elements must be balanced, but they must be balanced in different ways than psychometricians balance them in large-scale assessments. For example, two frequently discussed characteristics of assessments are reliability and validity. *Reliability* is the accuracy of a measurement; *validity* is the extent to which an assessment actually measures what it purports to measure (Marzano, 2018). Large-scale assessments have myriad processes, procedures, equations, and methods to create and preserve reliability and validity. The constructs of reliability and validity are still important in classroom assessments, but the ways teachers achieve them are different. The following sections highlight the potency of well-designed classroom assessments and the ways that proficiency scales ensure unidimensionality and validity, series of scores over time provide reliability, and parallel assessments yield comparable scores.

Proficiency Scales Ensure Unidimensionality and Validity

Unidimensionality means that an assessment should measure one thing; more formal definitions say that an assessment should measure "one dimension" of knowledge or skill. If you pause to think about this, it becomes almost self-evident. If an assessment assesses both a student's knowledge of a science standard and their ability to write, what does a proficient score on that assessment mean? Does it mean that the student is proficient in both skills? Or is it possible that they compensated for low science knowledge with exceptional writing skills? Or vice versa? It is difficult to tell. Therefore, unidimensionality dictates that either (1) an assessment measures only one dimension of knowledge or skill, or (2) multiple scores are assigned (one score per dimension) if an assessment measures more than one dimension of knowledge or skill (Marzano et al., 2017). For example, consider the cognitive skills described in the Nonacademic Outcomes section of chapter 2 (page 39). As Marzano and colleagues (2019) explained, these skills will almost always be assessed in the context of tasks involving academic content. When assigning scores for these tasks, "teachers would assign these tasks two scores—one representing students' understanding of the academic content and the other representing students' execution of the [nonacademic] process" (p. 93).

As described previously, *validity* means that an assessment actually measures what it purports to measure. It is a small step from unidimensionality to validity. Unidimensional assessments are likely to also be valid as long as the one dimension they are measuring has been clearly defined. Marzano (2018) explained:

> Since classroom assessments will generally focus on one topic or dimension over a relatively short period, teachers can more easily ensure that they have acceptable levels for validity. Indeed . . . some measurement experts contend that classroom assessments have such high levels of validity that we should not be concerned about their seemingly poor reliability. (p. 14)

We'll address the "poor reliability" of classroom assessments in the next section, but for now, let's talk about how to ensure both unidimensionality and validity in classroom assessments. The answer is proficiency scales, which provide the clarity needed to create unidimensional and valid classroom assessments. As Marzano and colleagues (2019) explained:

> Effective assessment begins with clarity regarding the content that will be the focus of instruction and assessment. To this end, we strongly recommend the use of proficiency scales to define specific learning goals (also known as learning targets) and various levels of proficiency relative to those goals. (p. vii)

Using proficiency scales allows for a valid and unidimensional assessment approach by providing targeted feedback on specific learning goals rather than assigning a single, overall grade. For example, if students have the opportunity to demonstrate their understanding of a science concept through an essay, infographic, or public service video, a teacher can apply distinct proficiency scales to evaluate their grasp of the science content separately from their communication skills in writing, visual design, or video production. Instead of a broad rubric that combines everything into one score, proficiency scales enable the teacher to give focused feedback on each specific dimension of learning, helping learners understand where they excel and where they can improve in both content knowledge and the medium of expression they chose.

Series of Scores Over Time Provide Reliability

As stated previously, reliability involves the accuracy of a measurement. Reliability is a significant challenge for large-scale assessment designers because they usually have only one chance per year to administer their large-scale assessment to students. Since all assessments involve error, and these assessments are administered only once, the designers need to go to great lengths to reduce that error as far as possible (Marzano et al., 2019). But for the classroom teacher designing classroom assessments, this challenge evaporates (Marzano et al., 2017; Marzano & Abbott, 2022).

There is no need for a classroom teacher to base a student's score on one single assessment; doing so imposes an unnecessary burden on classroom assessment systems. Classroom teachers can establish reliability simply by administering multiple assessments on a particular topic to students over time (Marzano, 2018). Marzano and colleagues (2019) explained that teachers often fail to leverage this powerful advantage of the classroom assessment context:

> As long as we think of tests as independent events, the scores from which educators must interpret in isolation, there is little hope for precision at the individual student level. However, if one changes the perspective from a single assessment to multiple assessments administered and interpreted over time, then it becomes not only possible but relatively straightforward to generate a relatively precise summary score for individuals. (p. 5)

If multiple assessments on a topic are parallel and yield comparable scores (as discussed in the next section), teachers can confidently draw inferences about a student's current status on that topic by looking at their series of scores on that topic collected over time. More scores translate to more reliability (Marzano et al., 2019).

Parallel Assessments Yield Comparable Scores

Assessments for collecting a series of scores that accurately indicate a student's current status on a topic must meet two criteria.

1. They must offer students the opportunity to demonstrate proficiency with all levels of a proficiency scale.
2. They must yield comparable scores.

Assessments that meet these criteria are typically called *parallel assessments*.

Relative to the first criterion, the items on parallel assessments must have equal levels of difficulty. In the same way that the proficiency scale articulates target, simpler, and more complex content, all parallel assessments must include opportunities for students to demonstrate proficiency with simpler, target, and more complex content from the proficiency scale (Marzano, 2018; Marzano et al., 2019). This does not preclude the possibility of quick checks to see whether a student has learned a specific element or level of a proficiency scale; teachers can and should do these quick checks, but they should not contribute to the series of scores used to determine a student's current status.

Relative to the second criterion, parallel assessments must all ultimately be scored using the same system. This does not mean that every assessment must be scored in exactly the same way; in fact, many assessments yield what Marzano and colleagues (2019) called *format-specific scores*. That simply means that every format-specific score must be eventually translated into the common scoring scheme. If you are using proficiency scales, this usually entails using a 0.0–4.0 scale. You can use other scoring approaches (100-point, letter grades, and so on), but the non-negotiable factor in using a series of scores to create reliability is that every assessment score must ultimately align with the same scoring scheme. This results in all assessments yielding comparable scores. Figure 5.2 illustrates this dynamic.

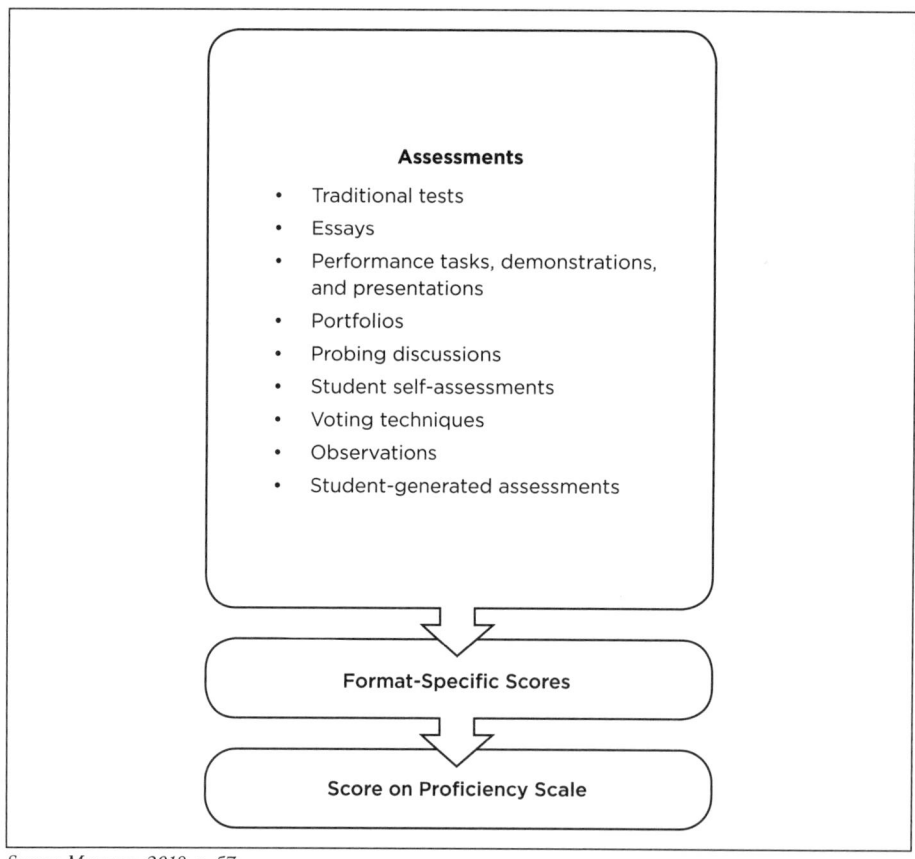

Source: Marzano, 2018, p. 57.
Figure 5.2: Translation of all scores into a common scoring scheme.

Notice that neither of the two criteria articulated here dictates that all the assessments used to collect scores need to be of the same type. In fact, as mentioned previously and as shown in figure 5.2, the wide variety of assessment types used to collect scores range from traditional pencil-and-paper tests to over-the-shoulder observations to student-generated assessments (Marzano & Kosena, 2022). To drive this point home, some schools adjust the language they use to refer to assessment. For example, educators in Westminster Public Schools use the term *evidence* instead of *assessment* to reinforce the idea that demonstration of proficiency can and should come in a variety of forms (Gotto et al., 2025). Marzano, Aschoff, and Avila (2022) made the following observation:

> *This wide array of types of classroom assessment is possible only because the content of the curriculum is explicitly stated as proficiency scales. In effect, when proficiency scales are available, the types of activities that qualify as assessments increase dramatically. (pp. 49-50)*

In sum, parallel assessments employ different items and different assessment formats, but they all measure the same measurement topic. The different types of assessments listed in figure 5.2 fall into four general categories: (1) obtrusive assessments, (2) unobtrusive assessments, (3) student-generated assessments, and (4) student self-assessments. We discuss each further in the following sections.

Obtrusive Assessments

Obtrusive assessments interrupt the flow of instruction (Marzano & Abbott, 2022). These might be traditional pencil-and-paper tests, online tests, probing discussions, demonstrations, presentations, or other performance assessments. Often, obtrusive assessments based on proficiency scales contain three sections (Marzano, 2018).

1. A section devoted to items measuring score 2.0 content
2. A section devoted to items measuring score 3.0 content
3. A section devoted to items measuring score 4.0 content

This is easy to conceptualize with a pencil-and-paper or online test; the test form simply contains three sections. If you are using a probing discussion, plan out questions that will allow you to systematically determine whether the student understands the 2.0 content, 3.0 content, and 4.0 content. As Marzano and colleagues (2019) explained, "Probably the most useful aspect of the probing discussion is that the teacher can ask students to clarify their answers if he or she needs more evidence to determine if they answered a question correctly" (p. 69). For example, the teacher can say while pointing to the proficiency scale, "Do you know this?" After the student answers, the teacher goes to the next level, saying, "Great! How do you see that knowledge fitting in with the other knowledge in the scale?" If you are using a performance assessment, such as a demonstration or presentation, you should build opportunities into the assessment for students to demonstrate score 2.0, score 3.0, and score 4.0 understanding of the content (Hayes et al., 2021).

One note of caution about obtrusive assessments: It's easy to lose unidimensionality if the assessment requires students to read, write, organize information, or use public speaking skills (such as eye contact or clarity of speech) when those skills are not the focus of the assessment. Lack of expertise with those skills can eclipse the students' performance with the measurement topic being assessed. Therefore, consider using a separate proficiency scale for reading, writing, presentation, or public speaking skills during obtrusive assessments; this allows you to give actionable feedback on these important skills while not confounding them with the true focus of the assessment.

Unobtrusive Assessments

Unobtrusive assessments gather information about a student's current status on a proficiency scale without interrupting the flow of instruction. These might be informal observations, conversations, or analyses of written products (such as learning logs or academic notebooks; Marzano, Aschoff, & Avila, 2022). By nature, these assessments increase the number of scores or amount of assessment evidence teachers can collect for each student without using instructional time for obtrusive assessments. Moreover, unobtrusive assessments are an excellent option if a teacher knows that test anxiety frequently interferes with a student's ability to demonstrate what they know. While test-anxious students do need to practice taking tests, anxiety can introduce levels of error that may skew the student's score and make the data collected less useful. Thus, unobtrusive assessments offer a vehicle to obtain more accurate and error-free scores for students who struggle with test anxiety (Marzano, Aschoff, & Avila, 2022).

For example, a teacher might use unobtrusive assessments during a small-group discussion on a new science concept, such as the water cycle. Rather than using a quiz, the teacher observes each student's contributions, noting how well they understand and use terms like *evaporation*, *condensation*, and *precipitation*. The teacher also takes note of questions the students ask, which provide insight into gaps in understanding. Later, the teacher may review the students' learning logs to see how they summarize the topic and apply it to real-life examples, such as rain formation. This combination of observations and written reflections provides a rich picture of each student's understanding without the pressure of a formal test.

Student-Generated Assessments

Possibly one of the most transformational ideas related to competency-based assessment systems involves empowering students to take responsibility for their learning, including demonstrating their learning through student-generated assessments. Marzano and colleagues (2017) explained, "When a student feels that she has achieved a particular level of proficiency, she goes to the teacher and explains how she will demonstrate her knowledge or skill" (p. 116). Student-generated assessments include the same wide range of choices as other types of assessments; they might be sets of questions with answers, artifacts, demonstrations, or discussions with the teacher.

One unique approach to student-generated assessment involves asking students to create assessment items that demonstrate their understanding of the content. Using a preexisting set of item templates—such as those provided by Robert J. Marzano, Christopher W. Dodson, Julia A. Simms, and Jacob P. Wipf (2022) in *Ethical Test Preparation in the Classroom*—students can create an assessment for a particular measurement topic. In an ELA classroom, the teacher might ask students to create several assessment items for determining an author's purpose after reading a set of three texts. The teacher provides the students with item templates that show the question structures typically used to assess understanding of author's purpose during large-scale assessments. For example, they might use the following item template, called a function frame.

> **How does [Textual Element] do [Literary Element]?**
>
> **[Textual Element] =** Character actions, thoughts, or words; a sentence; an event; a point of view; a picture; a literary device
>
> **[Literary Element] =** An important or main idea; an argument or purpose of the passage; the whole plot; the structure of the passage

Students practice filling in textual elements and literary elements from each of the texts in the set to create assessment items for determining author's purpose.

As any teacher who has written an assessment can attest, designing test items for content requires deep understanding and complex application of that knowledge. To further demonstrate their understanding of the content using a test they designed themselves, students might also have the opportunity to adjust the test items they wrote to make them easier or harder; students should also explain why their adjustments make the items easier or harder.

Student Self-Assessments

Student self-assessments are distinct from student-generated assessments. Whereas student-generated assessments are primarily designed for a teacher audience, student self-assessments are primarily designed for students to keep track of their own progress on specific proficiency scales. However, like student-generated assessments, student self-assessment tools communicate that "students have the right and the invitation to take major responsibility for how they are evaluated" (Marzano, Aschoff, & Avila, 2022, p. 199).

In traditional education systems, teachers often overlook the importance of student self-assessments, focusing instead on teacher-led evaluations and standardized tests. Self-assessment is rarely seen as an integral part of the assessment cycle, with many educators prioritizing external measures of student progress over encouraging students to reflect on their own learning. However, in a competency-based system, student self-assessment plays a critical role in helping learners take ownership of their progress, develop self-regulation skills, and identify areas for growth. This approach aligns with John Hattie's (2009) research, which places student self-reported grades at the top of the list for strategies that have the greatest impact on learning outcomes. By incorporating self-assessment into the learning process, competency-based systems empower students to become active participants in their own educational journey.

One of the simplest tools for student self-assessment is the personal tracking matrix (Marzano & Abbott, 2022). Figure 5.3 is an example of a personal tracking matrix for a health topic. Personal tracking matrixes serve both students and teachers. For students, they make status and growth visible and are easily updated as students progress. For teachers, they provide a quick window into students' self-ratings regarding their current status on a particular proficiency scale.

Marzano and Abbott (2022) explained that each individual learning target from a proficiency scale gets a row in the personal tracking matrix. For each target, students rate their understanding using the scale at the top of the matrix.

- I'm still confused about this topic.
- I've learned some but not all of the topic.
- I've got this now.

Level	Indicator	My Rating			My Evidence
		I'm still confused about this topic.	I've learned some but not all of the topic.	I've got this now.	
4	I can show examples of different types of diets and explain how they might affect a person's body.				
3	I can explain what eating different types of foods might do to my body.				
2	I can explain foods that are in a balanced diet.				
2	I can read and explain a food label.				
2	I can give examples of fad diets and explain why they are not always healthy choices.				
2	I can give examples of unhealthy foods using the Dietary Guidelines for Americans.				
2	I can give examples of healthy foods using the Dietary Guidelines for Americans.				
2	I can explain the term *dietary guidelines*.				
2	I can explain the term *fad*.				
2	I can explain the term *additive*.				
2	I can explain the term *nutrition*.				
2	I can explain the term *calorie*.				
2	I can explain the term *protein*.				
2	I can explain the term *carbohydrate*.				
2	I can explain the term *sodium*.				

Source: Marzano & Kosena, 2022, p. 130. Adapted from Marzano, 2017.
Figure 5.3: Personal tracking matrix for a health topic.

Possibly the most important column in a personal tracking matrix appears on the far right, labeled *My Evidence*. Here, students record the evidence that supports their assertion about their progress; this evidence is especially important for targets where the student says, "I've got this now." This evidence allows the teacher to use the personal tracking matrix as an assessment tool as well. Marzano and colleagues (2017) explained further:

> *For the teacher to use the matrix as an assessment, the student would have to provide more evidence for the score he assigned. This evidence might be in a folder the student keeps with related assignments and assessments or evidence that has been archived electronically. The teacher would examine the student's self-assessment represented in the personal tracking matrix and the supporting evidence and translate it into a proficiency scale score. The personal tracking matrix analysis often accompanies a brief conversation with the student. (p. 116)*

Student self-assessments, such as the personal tracking matrix, foster greater student ownership of learning and enhance students' ability to track and reflect on their process. Student self-assessments also provide valuable information to teachers and opportunities for both students and teachers to check the accuracy of their current conceptions of a learner's knowledge and skill.

Scoring and Grading

As stated previously, a student's current status on a proficiency scale should never be determined by a single assessment. Instead, teachers should collect a series of scores to infer a score representing the student's current status. This inferred score (based on a series of scores) is referred to as the student's *summative score*. The individual scores within the series of scores are referred to as the student's *formative scores*. Marzano and colleagues (2017) further explained the distinction:

> *At any point in time, every student should have a score indicating his or her current status on each measurement topic. . . . Scores (not assessments) should be thought of as formative or summative. At some point in time, a teacher must assign a summative score to a student. All the preceding scores are considered formative. (p. 122)*

Note that, given the flexibility built into a competency-based assessment system, not all students will have the exact same number of formative scores for a specific measurement topic (Marzano, Aschoff, & Avila, 2022). While all students might take several common obtrusive assessments, it is likely that the teacher will record varying numbers of unobtrusive or student-generated assessment scores for each student. This is not a problem.

When synthesizing a series of formative scores to infer a summative score, there are several different approaches, as Marzano, Aschoff, and Avila (2022) demonstrated:

- **Average:** *Gives equal weight to each evidence score, in effect assuming that little, if any, learning has occurred over the time the teacher scored assessments.*

- **Linear trend:** Computed under the assumption that students learn at a constant rate.... Means that students learn as much from week 1 to week 2 as they do from week 2 to week 3 and so on.

- **Power-law trend:** Depicted by the curved line that flattens out over time.... Computed under the assumption that students learn quickly in the beginning, but when they get to the more complex content at the higher levels of a proficiency scale, their rate of learning slows down or flattens. (p. 47)

In general, psychometricians and theorists discourage educators from using the average to compute a summative score. Harrison (2020) explained this as follows:

> When calculating a ... grade from a set of scores within a single content standard, **averaging is likely a poor choice**. There are better models that capture student performance, such as trend awareness and variations of the power law formula, as explained thoroughly in educational research literature. (p. 4)

The linear trend and power law are typically better choices for evaluating trends in sets of student formative scores.

Each of these approaches can be done either by hand or using mathematical models (which often occur within a learning management system programmed with appropriate algorithms). But in most cases, a teacher's judgment is at least as accurate as the conclusions drawn by algorithmic models. For example, a teacher reviews a student's formative scores on a measurement topic to determine the most accurate summative score. If, over a six-week period, a student has demonstrated for a measurement topic the score pattern of 1.0, 2.0, 2.5, 2.0, 3.0, 3.0, 3.5, and 3.0, it is quite easy to see that their current summative score is somewhere between 3.0 and 3.5, and likely closer to 3.0. Either way, the goal when inferring a summative score is to answer the question Marzano and colleagues (2019) asked: "Given this pattern of scores, what is the most reasonable estimate of the student's current summative score?" (p. 80).

This discussion highlights an important bedrock of competency-based assessment practices, according to Marzano and Abbott (2022): "The teacher is the final judge as to whether or not students have demonstrated proficiency" (p. 151). This means that the teacher is not beholden to or limited by one specific score that a student achieved on one particular assessment (as is sometimes the case in traditional assessment systems). Rather, the teacher uses their judgment to determine the summative score that best represents the student's current status. If the teacher isn't sure, they simply collect more evidence from the student and add an additional score using one of the myriad assessment types available. This is the heart of reassessment.

Recall that we began our discussion of classroom assessment design by highlighting the flexibility of classroom assessment. The same flexibility is a key to offering true reassessment opportunities. Reassessment does not mean students taking the same test until they pass; this can lead to students not taking the first administration of a test seriously, or using it as an opportunity to preview the test so they know what to study. True reassessments occur when the format and questions of an assessment are flexed to provide an additional opportunity (or opportunities) for students to demonstrate mastery of the outcomes. Teachers should continue to reassess and collect additional data until they are confident that the summative score they assign accurately represents that student's current level of knowledge and skill for a particular measurement topic.

Data Notebooks

Students should know their status on any specific measurement topic at any time. While students can engage in self-assessment using personal tracking matrixes, they should also have access to their series of formative scores and be aware of the current summative score the teacher has computed for them on each of the measurement topics they are currently working on. Data notebooks are an excellent tool to this end (Marzano & Abbott, 2022).

Whether data notebooks are kept electronically or on paper in a binder, they might include the following elements, detailed by Marzano and Kosena (2022), in addition to formative and summative scores for each measurement topic the student is working on.

- **Assessment data:** Preassessment and benchmark assessment data can help students identify which learning targets to work on.

- **Descriptions of learning targets:** These can include the description from the original proficiency scale, the description from a student-friendly proficiency scale, or the student's interpretation of the expectations on the proficiency scale. Teachers should review these descriptions for accuracy of interpretation.

- **Vocabulary lists:** Students can track the terms (and their descriptions of those terms) that underlie the knowledge and skills for each specific learning target.

- **Learning action plans:** This is a space for students to set goals and articulate what they must do to demonstrate mastery of each learning target.

- **Reflections:** This element prompts students to write about their progress, challenges they have met, how they overcame those challenges, and strategies for continued improvement.

For example, in a seventh-grade mathematics class, a student sits down with her data notebook at the beginning of her weekly self-assessment session. She starts by reviewing her progress on her current learning targets in mathematics. The teacher has decided to create a digital notebook containing a personalized matrix to track the student's formative scores on various measurement topics. The student sees that her formative scores for fractions have steadily improved over the past month, and her current summative score reflects her hard work. She clicks on a link to take her to the Learning Targets section, where she reviews a student-friendly description of her next goal in geometry. In the Vocabulary List section, she adds definitions for the terms *perpendicular* and *bisect*.

After noting her progress, the student opens the Learning Action Plan and sets a goal to master constructing geometric shapes by the end of the week. She lists the specific steps she plans to take, such as completing extra practice problems and then asking her teacher to assess her current level so she can receive feedback for improvement. Finally, she reflects on her journey so far in the Reflections section. She writes about her initial struggles with fractions, how she practiced regularly to improve, and her excitement about moving on to geometry. This reflective exercise is designed to help the student understand her own learning process, motivating her to keep working toward mastery.

Summary

Assessment is central to implementing competency-based practices. For both feedback and measurement purposes, assessment systems must be valid, reliable, and flexible. Retakes and self-assessment are critical components that build on the structural aspects of student agency and equity discussed in chapters 3 (page 59) and 4 (page 75). Synthesizing multiple assessment scores over time into a summative score should be done using methods that assume student learning over time. Such assessment systems provide meaningful and actionable feedback that empowers students to monitor their own progress and take control of their learning.

CHAPTER 6

Instruction

Almost every researcher, practitioner, and theorist who writes about competency-based practices agrees: Instruction looks different in a competency-based classroom. These differences typically revolve around the two following aspects of competency-based practices that manifest strongly during instructional time.

1. Students move through the content at different paces and are, therefore, working on different topics at any one point in time.
2. Teachers no longer focus primarily on teaching but instead focus on how learners are interacting with and understanding the content.

Making these changes to instruction necessitates making changes to the way teachers plan for instruction. Importantly, while teachers will always need time for independent planning, collaborative planning can yield benefits to a school implementing competency-based practices. With that in mind, there are three questions that guide a school's decision making about instruction and planning.

1. How will we carry out instructional planning?
2. What grouping structures will we use to present content to students?
3. What instructional resources and approaches will we use?

In this chapter, we consider options and offer guidance to assist you in making decisions about each.

Instructional Unit Design

Researcher Peter J. McPherson (2021) found that collaboration and teamwork were crucial to the success of teachers and administrators implementing competency-based practices. Evans and colleagues (2019) also studied competency-based practice implementations and identified professional learning communities as a high-leverage practice with the potential to drive whole system reform. According to Robert J. Marzano, Tammy Heflebower, Jan K. Hoegh, Phil Warrick, and Gavin Grift (2016), a *professional learning community* is "a schoolwide system of teacher teams that collaborate on issues of instruction, assessment, and other school topics with the goal of improving student learning" (p. 3). Such a system can be used very productively for instructional planning, especially common unit design.

Common unit design in the context of a professional learning community lays a robust foundation for one of the most important elements of competency-based practice implementation: collective responsibility. As Marzano and Kosena (2022) explained, "Instead of individual teachers making their own curricular decisions and creating their own idiosyncratic unit plans, teams of teachers collectively engage in this activity" (p. 150). Common unit design and planning help ensure that students receive well-designed instruction regardless of which teacher they are learning with. They also enable a system in which all educators in a school share responsibility for the learning of all students.

Additionally, common designing and planning at the unit level, rather than the lesson level, give each teacher flexibility regarding how to craft daily lessons to meet the specific needs of their students. Working at the unit level rather than the lesson level also helps teachers plan with an appropriate level of specificity. Teachers should not spend their time planning every daily move; too much investment in these carefully laid plans can prevent teachers from flexibly adjusting when data indicate that students need something different. Instead, we recommend that planning and unit design involve the following seven elements across a unit, which are also part of *The New Art and Science of Teaching* model (Marzano, 2017).

1. Chunking
2. Previewing
3. Recording and representing
4. Processing and practicing
5. Undertaking projects and complex tasks
6. Generating and defending claims
7. Reviewing and revising

Here, we review each element and provide guidance about how to plan for it and incorporate it into instruction.

Chunking

Whenever they encounter new content, students are at risk of being overwhelmed. Chunking is an essential process for overcoming the limitations of working memory. As Marzano and Abbott (2022) explained, failing to plan for chunking can cause students to perceive new information as "a cacophony that results in very little overall understanding" (p. 71). According to Marzano, Aschoff, and Avila (2022), teachers must help students identify two things about new content: (1) the relative importance of each chunk of information and (2) an organizational scheme that groups related chunks of content together

Proficiency scales, by their very nature, facilitate content chunking. Each target at each level represents a potential chunk; teachers should evaluate these during planning to see if they are too large or too small. And the progression of the proficiency scale presents a starting point for teachers as they decide the order to present chunks. Typically, smaller and simpler chunks at the 2.0 level of a proficiency scale are presented first, followed by chunks at the 3.0 and 4.0 levels.

As collaborative teams of teachers engage in planning for chunks of content, they should allow the content's complexity to guide their decisions about how big each chunk should be. As Marzano and Abbott (2022) explained, more complex content should be presented in smaller chunks. The chunks can be larger if the information is less complex. It is important to note that *less complex* does not mean easy or less important. Instead, it means that the content is more straightforward with fewer variables, layers of meaning, or nuanced relationships that require careful analysis and comprehension. Additionally, educators must consider students' background knowledge. If new content is being presented to students who have plenty of related background knowledge, the chunk size can be larger; conversely, the chunk size needs to be smaller for students with limited background knowledge. Once teachers have determined chunk size, they will need to plan for what happens before, during, and after presenting each chunk. In other words, teachers will need to plan for previewing, recording and representing information, and processing and practicing information, the focus of the next three sections.

Previewing

Once teachers have appropriately chunked content for a specific group of students, they should plan activities that will help students preview each chunk of new knowledge (Marzano, Aschoff, & Avila, 2022). Effective previewing activities share the common features of activating students' background knowledge and preparing students to build mental models or images of new content (Marzano & Abbott, 2022). For example, at the elementary level, before students learn about the phases of the moon, the teacher can help students activate background knowledge by completing a concept map to organize what they already know about the moon or by showing images of different phases of the moon and asking students to discuss what they notice about the images. At the secondary level, the teacher might provide students with the proficiency scale and a worksheet that asks them to separate the content knowledge in the scale into two different columns—one for what they already know and the other for what they do not know. It can also include a reflective question such as "Of the content I do not know, what am I going to do to move my thinking forward?" This allows students to activate prior knowledge while also increasing the likelihood they will be motivated to fill the gap in their knowledge. Awareness of not knowing is one way to motivate humans to learn; we do not like not knowing.

A previewing activity that's useful at all levels is generate-sort-connect. In this technique, students brainstorm everything they know about a particular topic. Students then use an affinity diagram (often created using sticky notes) to categorize their background knowledge and draw connections between categories. This process often leads students to generate questions that they want to answer as they learn the new content.

Similarly, anticipation guides provide students with statements related to the upcoming content and ask them to agree or disagree with each statement. For example, figure 6.1 shows an anticipation guide for a unit on ratios and percentages.

In a visual twist on anticipation guides, picture walks involve displaying images, diagrams, and animations related to the upcoming content around the room. In small groups, students rotate around the room, and at each station, they share their thoughts with a partner. Then, the class reconvenes, and students share their thoughts with the whole class.

Read each statement and decide if you agree or disagree.	
Statement	**Agree/Disagree**
1. A ratio compares two quantities and shows how much there is of one item for each unit of another.	*Agree/Disagree*
2. Ratios and fractions are completely different and should not be used in the same way.	*Agree/Disagree*
3. A percentage is another way to represent a fraction or ratio.	*Agree/Disagree*
4. If two recipes use the same ingredients but in different ratios, they will taste the same.	*Agree/Disagree*
5. Percentages are useful only when working with money.	*Agree/Disagree*
6. To find 25 percent of a number, you can divide the number by 4.	*Agree/Disagree*
7. You can use equivalent ratios to solve problems in real life, like creating a recipe or mixing paint.	*Agree/Disagree*
8. A ratio of 3:5 is the same as saying 60 percent to 40 percent.	*Agree/Disagree*
9. Doubling both terms in a ratio will change the meaning of the ratio.	*Agree/Disagree*
10. To find the percentage of a quantity, multiply by the percentage and divide by 100.	*Agree/Disagree*

Figure 6.1: Anticipation guide for ratios and percentages.

Recording and Representing

As teachers plan for unit design, they need to build opportunities for students to record and represent new content. Recording and representing activities serve two important learning functions. First, for learners to write about (record) or create images and models (represent) of new content, they must recall that content. Cognitive psychologist Shana K. Carpenter (2023) confirmed that each time students bring content from long-term memory back into working memory, it strengthens their memory of it. As neuroscientists Cathy Rogers and Michael S. C. Thomas (2023) reinforced, "The act of retrieving, enabling working memory to reactivate information within long-term memory systems, means relearning it" (p. 127).

Second, using two channels (words and images) to express content allows students to harness more of their working memory than is available using a single channel. Therefore, asking students to express new content using both words and images or mental models allows them to incorporate more new content into long-term memory than would otherwise be practicable (Marzano, Aschoff, & Avila, 2022).

As conveyed at the outset of chapter 5 (page 89), in the context of assessment, recording and representing allow for the invisible processes of thinking to become visible so the teacher can provide the necessary feedback to help students improve their thinking. While teachers often use recording and representing strategies in traditional classrooms, competency-based classrooms and teachers often adjust the type of recording and representation for the individual learner or small group of students. If the goal is to help students record and represent the new content chunk shared, they should use a strategy that works for them.

Processing and Practicing

Once students have received chunks of knowledge and had the opportunity to record and represent them, they need opportunities to process and practice their new learning. Processing and practicing knowledge involves receiving, interpreting, storing, and retrieving that knowledge in a structured manner. According to Marzano (2017), after learners receive a manageable chunk of information, they should engage in activities to process and internalize it. In competency-based classrooms, these activities often happen in small groups, allowing students to connect new knowledge with what they already know, building deeper understanding. Structured processing and practice time are crucial for teachers to see students' cognitive engagement, which is made visible through activities that produce artifacts of thought, such as written reflections or shared insights during discussions.

As Marzano, Aschoff, and Avila (2022) explained, "The act of processing needs to be purposeful and structured. Rather than simply putting students in pairs or small groups and vaguely prompting them to talk about the content, the teacher should use structured collaborative activities" (p. 54). To select appropriate processing activities for new knowledge, teachers will need to first identify the nature of that knowledge. Knowledge can be thought about in two categories: (1) declarative knowledge, which consists of information or "things we know," and (2) procedural knowledge, which consists of skills or "things we do."

Declarative Knowledge

When knowledge is declarative, common processing activities include summarizing, questioning, and predicting. Summarizing allows students to condense key ideas, questioning helps them identify gaps in their understanding, and predicting encourages students to use existing knowledge to anticipate new concepts. Additionally, examining similarities and differences between new knowledge and existing knowledge can help students process and deepen new declarative knowledge.

Activities that involve examining similarities and differences typically take four primary forms: (1) comparing, (2) classifying, (3) creating metaphors, and (4) creating analogies (Marzano & Abbott, 2022). The simplest form is *comparison* activities. These involve determining characteristics by which to compare two or more informational items, identifying how the items are similar or different for each characteristic, and drawing conclusions based on the comparison.

Another activity that involves similarities and differences is *classification*. During classification activities, students identify categories to which items belong and group items according to categories. Classification activities usually follow a process where students address questions such as the following:

1. *What item am I thinking about?*
2. *What category does the item fit into? What characteristics of the item lead me to this conclusion?*
3. *What are some other items that might be in the same category?*
4. *What do these other items tell me about my original item? (Marzano, Aschoff, & Avila, 2022, p. 69)*

Figure 6.2 shows a knowledge map useable for classification activities.

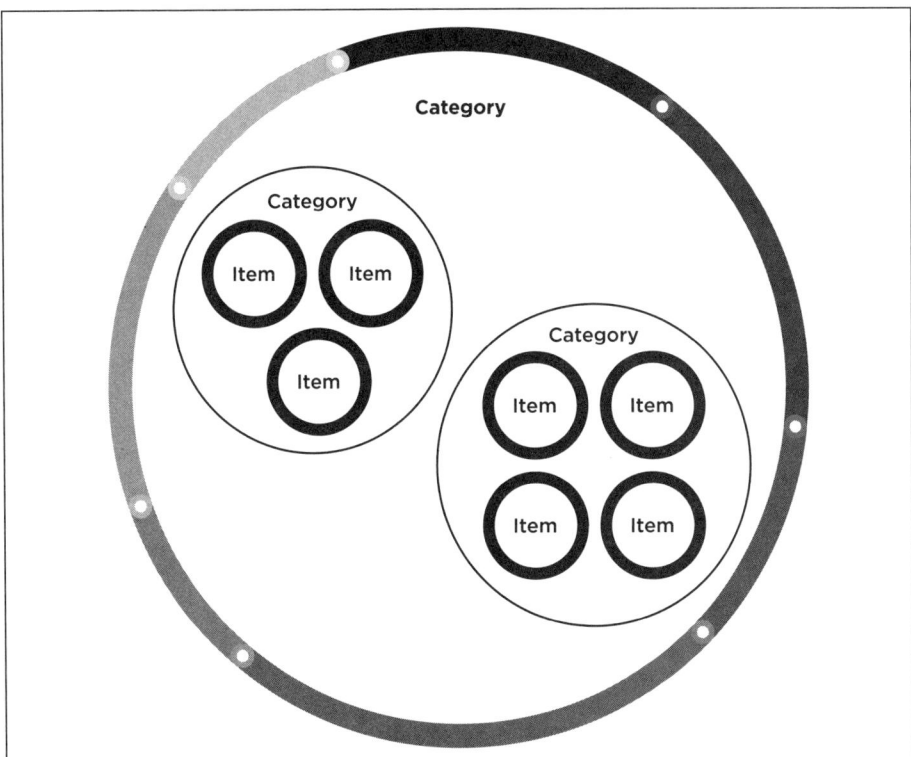

Source: © 2017 by Marzano Resources. Used with permission.
Figure 6.2: Knowledge map for classification activities.

Additional activities that involve similarities and differences include asking students to create *metaphors* and *analogies*. For example, when learning about the branches of government, students might generate metaphors between each branch and an aspect of their daily lives. When learning about the parts of a cell and their functions, students can create an analogy, comparing the parts of a cell to the parts of another system, such as a school, city, or home. Figure 6.3 and figure 6.4 present knowledge maps useable for activities that involve creating metaphors and analogies.

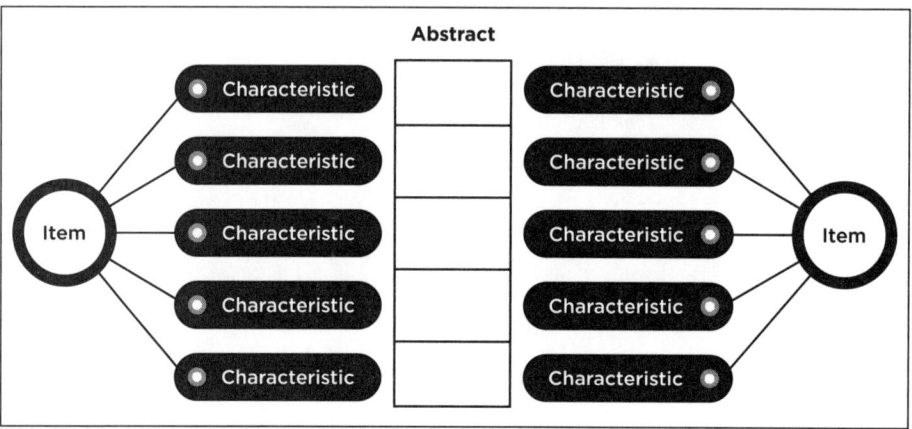

Source: © 2017 by Marzano Resources. Used with permission.
Figure 6.3: Knowledge map for creating metaphors.

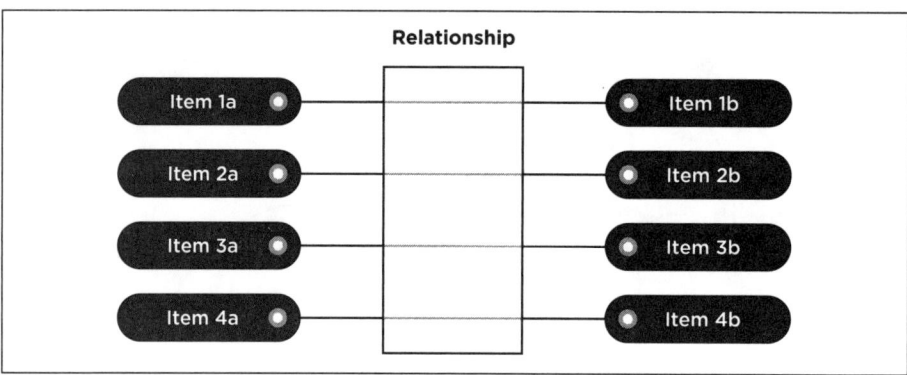

Source: © 2017 by Marzano Resources. Used with permission.
Figure 6.4: Knowledge map for creating analogies.

Activities that prompt students to process new information by examining similarities and differences provide opportunities for students to "interact with others about the content, analyze what they have just learned, and determine how it relates to what they already know" (Marzano & Abbott, 2022, p. 43).

Procedural Knowledge

As mentioned previously, not all knowledge is declarative. Some knowledge involves skills or strategies. This set of knowledge is known as *procedural knowledge*. To deepen skills and strategies, students must practice them (Marzano, Aschoff, & Avila, 2022). This practice should be structured and should progress through two phases. First, students should practice the skill or process slowly, focusing on accuracy and ensuring that they are correctly performing each step of the process and not leaving out any steps. Second, once students have gained confidence with their execution of the process and the teacher has confirmed that they are performing it without errors or omissions, students can transition to fluency practice. During this type of practice, the focus is on gaining speed and automaticity while preserving accuracy; teachers often use timed practice, online games, or speed challenges for this type of practice.

For example, when learners begin to develop an understanding of dividing fractions, they need to be told the steps for successfully implementing the strategies. Once the learners know the steps, they begin putting them together to divide simple fractions. The teacher should show them worked examples and provide modeling; students might complete partially solved problems with missing steps. As students are repeatedly able to apply the process to divide fractions accurately, it is appropriate for them to begin to tweak the procedure to see what works best for them. Finally, once they can consistently use the process, students engage in repeated practice to develop fast and fluent execution of the process. As another example, when students are first learning to use geographic tools to identify, locate, and describe places in the western hemisphere, they should work slowly to ensure they follow each step and use the tools' features, such as the map key. Once they can perform these steps, students practice independently and work on building fluency with the tools.

Undertaking Projects and Complex Tasks

Competency-based classrooms usually involve project-based learning (Colby, 2017; Pane, Steiner, Baird, & Hamilton, 2015; Scheopner Torres et al., 2018). *Project-based learning* is a fairly broad label and can include capstone projects, personal projects, interest-based projects, and other approaches. Sutherland and Strunk (2021) described project-based learning as "a teaching method through which students gain knowledge and skills by working for an extended period to investigate and respond to an authentic and engaging question, problem, or challenge" (p. 12).

Commonalities among various manifestations of project-based learning include typically being interdisciplinary, aligning with standards and measurement topics, applying real-world skills such as problem solving and decision making, and offering ways for students to demonstrate their learning through performance (Education Policy Innovation Collaborative, 2021). As an example of project-based learning, Sutherland and Strunk (2021) described how, in one competency-based classroom, students compiled urban dictionaries to explore learning targets related to connotation, denotation, and etymology.

Capstone projects are a particular kind of project-based learning activity. According to Marzano and colleagues (2017), they are based on students' areas of interest and typically occur over the course of a school year. Within a specific academic domain (such as mathematics, art, music, science, health, physical education, social studies, English language arts, and so on), the student selects a specific issue that interests them (Marzano & Hardy, 2023). Then, the student engages in a specific complex task related to that issue. According to Marzano (2017), "Cognitively complex tasks require a number of mental steps for students. They also require using content in new ways" (p. 47). Table 6.1 presents six types of complex tasks that students might engage in as part of a capstone project.

Table 6.1: Complex Tasks and Associated Steps

Task	Steps
Decision Making: Generating and applying criteria to select between alternatives that appear equal	Consider the decision you are presented with. *What am I trying to decide?*
	Consider the alternatives provided to you and clarify anything you don't understand. *What are my choices?*
	Identify the criteria you will use to select among alternatives. *What are the important criteria for making my decision?*
	Determine the extent to which each alternative possesses each criterion using *not at all, somewhat,* and *a lot. How well does each of my choices match my criteria?*
	Determine which alternative possesses the most criteria, which is your decision. *Which choice matches best with the criteria?*
Problem Solving: Overcoming obstacles or constraints to achieve a goal	Consider the goal you are being asked to accomplish. *What am I trying to accomplish?*
	Consider the constraints or limiting conditions that you have been presented with and clarify anything you don't understand. *What are the limits or barriers that are in my way?*
	Determine how the constraints or limiting conditions are interfering with your ability to accomplish your goal. *How are the limits or barriers keeping me from my goal?*
	For each constraint or limiting condition, identify alternative ways of overcoming it. *What are some solutions for overcoming the limits or barriers?*

Task	Steps
continued	Identify and try out the alternative that appears to be the best. *Which solution will I try?*
	Evaluate the effectiveness of the alternatives you have tried and, if necessary, try a different alternative or identify additional ways of overcoming the constraints or limiting conditions. *How well did it work? Should I try another solution?*
Invention: Creating a new process or product that meets a specific identified need	**Phase I: Selection**
	Consider the situation you've been asked to make better or the thing you've been asked to invent. *What do I want to make, or what do I want to make better?*
	Seek clarity regarding what the invention should look like when you are done and the specific purpose it will fulfill. *What standards do I want to set up for my invention?*
	Phase II: Drafting
	Consider the standards your invention must meet and clarify any confusion. *How will I know my invention is successful?*
	Make a sketch, a model, or a rough draft of your invention. *What is the best way to make a rough draft of my invention?*
	Start developing your invention and think in terms of small steps that build on one another. *What steps do I need to take to move forward?*
	Occasionally but systematically step back and look at your invention as a whole to make sure all the parts work together to accomplish your purpose. *Does my invention meet the standards I have set?*
	Phase III: Revising
	Try your invention in different situations and note what works well and what doesn't work well. *How can I improve on my rough draft?*
	Stop when you feel that your invention has accomplished your initial purpose and has met the standards you have set for it. *Is my invention finished?*
Experimental Inquiry: Generating a hypothesis about a physical or psychological phenomenon and then testing the hypothesis	Make observations of the situation the teacher has identified. *What do I see or notice?*
	Describe what you have observed while trying to be as concrete and objective as possible. *What is the best way to tell about what I see or notice?*
	Consider the teacher's explanation of what happened. *What specific theories or rules did the teacher provide?*
	Based on the explanation, make a prediction. *What do I predict based on the explanation?*
	Set up an experiment or activity to test your prediction. *How can I test my prediction?*
	Explain the results of your experiment or activity using the teacher's explanation. *What happened? Is this what I predicted?*
	Describe any changes you would make in the teacher's explanation or any question you have about the teacher's explanation. *Do I need to try a different explanation?*

continued →

Task	Steps
Investigation: Identifying and then resolving differences of opinion or contradictory information about concepts, historical events, or future possible events	Clarify the question you have been provided with. *What event or idea do I want to explain?*
	Examine the information provided by the teacher about your topic. *What do people already know?*
	Using the information provided by the teacher, summarize what you already know about your topic. *What is the best way to tell about what people already know?*
	Describe something that people seem to be confused about or something people have different opinions on. *What confusions do people have about the idea or event?*
	Describe how you would clear up the confusion or the differences in opinion and, if necessary, collect more information to support your resolution. *What suggestions do I have for clearing up these confusions? How can I defend my suggestions?*
Systems Analysis: Describing and analyzing the parts of a system with particular emphasis on the relationships among the parts	Identify the parts of the system provided by the teacher. *What are the parts of my system?*
	Identify the boundaries of the system. *What are the things that are related to the system but are not part of it?*
	Draw a picture to show how the parts work together within the system. *How do the parts affect each other?*
	Describe what would happen if the parts involved in the interaction provided by the teacher stopped working. *What would happen if various parts stopped or changed their behavior?*

Source: Marzano & Abbott, 2022; Marzano, Aschoff, & Avila, 2022; Marzano Resources, 2017.

Personal projects are a different kind of project-based learning activity. They can be as long or as short as necessary but typically last less than an entire school year. According to Marzano (2019), personal projects follow a specific seven-step process.

1. **Identify a goal you want to accomplish:** For example, a middle schooler might want to improve their fitness and be able to run a mile without stopping.

2. **Find others who have accomplished the same goal (role models) and people who will support you (mentors):** For example, the student might identify a friend who runs track as a role model and their gym teacher as a mentor.

3. **Research the skills and resources needed to accomplish your goal:** For example, the student might need to build endurance through consistent exercise, learn how to pace themselves while running, and get appropriate gear such as comfortable running shoes.

4. **Figure out what you need to change about your behavior to achieve your goal:** For example, the student might need to stop watching a favorite show to have time to exercise each day.

5. **Design a plan to achieve your goal that specifies what you need to do now, what you will need to do later, and how hard you will need to work:** For example, the student's plan might include doing cardio exercises every other day for at least fifteen minutes to build stamina, gradually increasing the time and distance of their runs each week, and getting advice from their mentor on good warm-up and cool-down techniques.

6. **Highlight three small steps you need to take now:** For example, the student could (a) run for at least five minutes without stopping this week, (b) stretch before and after each run, and (c) track their exercise using a fitness app.

7. **Consider your progress by explaining what you've learned about yourself and your goal:** For example, after a few weeks, the student might realize that they are able to run longer distances than they thought they could, but that they still need to work on pushing through moments when they feel tired. They might also realize that sticking to a routine helps them stay motivated to exercise.

Personal projects are differentiated from other types of project-based learning because the focus of the project is selected by the student, the student designs the project, and the student implements the project. When personal projects are focused on altruistic ends, such as solving a community problem, they have the potential to help students experience self-actualization and transcendence, the highest levels of Maslow's hierarchy (Maslow, 1943, 1954, 1969, 1970).

Generating and Defending Claims

One of the most rigorous activities that teachers can use for processing new information is to have students generate and defend claims about the new information. For students to be successful at generating and defending claims, teachers will have to explain the nature of claims and the structure of evidence (Marzano & Abbott, 2022).

Katie Rogers and Julia A. Simms (2015) suggested that the teacher begin by explaining the differences between facts and opinions, as table 6.2 (page 122) shows.

Table 6.2: Examples of Fact and Opinion

Term	Definition	Examples
Fact	A statement that can be verified and confirmed	Colorado became the thirty-eighth state in the United States on August 1, 1876.
		At sea level on Earth, water boils at 212 degrees Fahrenheit.
		Abraham Lincoln delivered the Gettysburg Address on Thursday, November 19, 1863.
		In 2013, the film *Argo* won the Academy Award for Best Picture.
Opinion	A statement with which others may agree or disagree	Colorado is the best place to live in the United States.
		Hot water is never pleasant to drink.
		Abraham Lincoln was the most eloquent of all the U.S. presidents.
		Argo did not deserve the 2013 Academy Award for Best Picture.

Source: Rogers & Simms, 2015, p. 16.

Students need to understand that claims are opinions that they can support with evidence. Typically, evidence is provided using grounds, backing, and qualifiers. Table 6.3 gives definitions and examples of each.

Table 6.3: Four Elements of an Argument

Element	Definition	Example
Claim	A new idea or opinion. A claim may simply present information or suggest that certain action is needed.	Students should attend school year-round.
Grounds	The initial evidence—or reasoning—for a claim. Grounds are answers to the question, "Why do you think your claim is true?"	Over the summer, students forget what they learned in school.
Backing	Information or facts about grounds that help establish their validity. In some cases, backing is simply a more in-depth discussion of the grounds.	Karl L. Alexander, Doris R. Entwisle, and Linda Steffel Olson (2007) found that during the school year, the academic growth of low-income students was comparable to that of other students. They reported that gaps in achievement actually occurred over the summer.
Qualifiers	Exceptions to claims that indicate the degree of certainty for the claim.	Year-round schooling may not be the only solution to this opportunity deficit for low-income students.

Source: Rogers & Simms, 2015, p. 18.

Finally, teachers can show students how effective arguments are typically structured, as shown in figure 6.5.

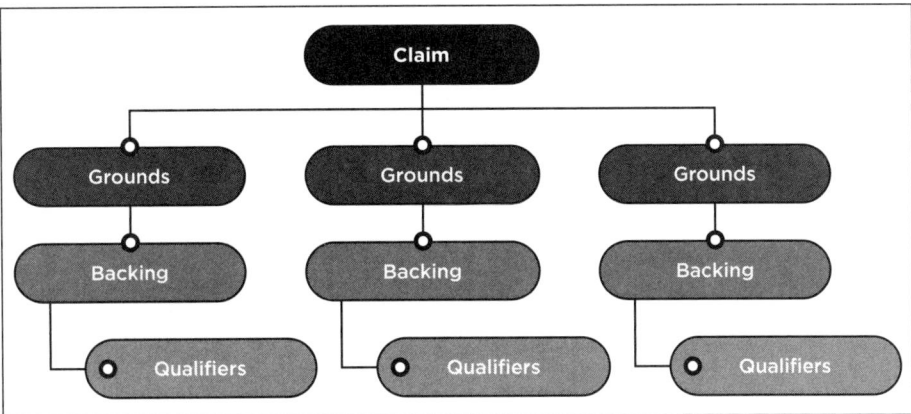

Source: Rogers & Simms, 2015, p. 22. Adapted from Toulmin, 2003.
Figure 6.5: Organization of an effective argument.

As an example of an activity for generating and defending claims, imagine a science lesson where students are learning about the effects of different variables on plant growth. The teacher begins by discussing facts and opinions using examples from the topic. Here, the facts include "Plants need sunlight to perform photosynthesis" and "Water is necessary for plants to absorb nutrients from the soil." Opinions might include "Cacti are the easiest plants to grow" and "Plants grown in natural sunlight are healthier than those grown under artificial lights."

After discussing the difference between facts and opinions, the teacher moves on to explain that claims are opinions that can be supported by evidence. For example, if a student claims, "Plants grow faster when they receive more sunlight," the student can support this claim by gathering evidence through experiments.

The teacher then introduces the four elements of an argument using the same topic.

1. **Claim:** A statement or opinion to be proven—for example, "Plants exposed to six hours of direct sunlight daily will grow taller than plants exposed to three hours."

2. **Grounds:** Facts or data that support the claim—for example, "In our experiment, plants with six hours of sunlight grew an average of five centimeters taller over four weeks compared to those with only three hours."

3. **Backing:** Additional support for the grounds, often using research or authoritative sources—for example, "According to a study published in the journal *Plant Biology*, plants exposed to more sunlight tend to have higher rates of photosynthesis, leading to increased growth."

4. **Qualifier:** Conditions or limits to the claim, acknowledging exceptions or boundaries—for example, "This claim is based on observations of a specific type of plant in controlled indoor conditions and may not apply to all plant species or outdoor environments."

Finally, the teacher can demonstrate the typical structure of an argument using a visual diagram. For example, a graphic organizer might illustrate how to introduce a claim, present supporting evidence (grounds and backing), and include qualifiers to strengthen the argument.

Reviewing and Revising

One of the strongest characteristics of competency-based practices is their emphasis on continuous improvement. Students are constantly being urged and supported to improve their performance on the topics and outcomes of the curriculum. This improvement is not always the result of new learning; in many cases, students upgrade their knowledge through review and revision processes. Therefore, during unit design and planning, teachers should build in systematic opportunities for students to engage in structured review and revision activities (Marzano, Aschoff, & Avila, 2022).

One of the most effective ways to engage students in structured review and revision is a strategy known as *cumulative review*. According to Marzano, Aschoff, and Avila (2022), the process has three phases.

1. **Recording:** Students record what they remember about a specific topic.

2. **Reviewing:** Students analyze what they have recorded to examine and test their understanding of the content, responding to prompts such as the following.

    a. Provide more details about what you recorded.

    b. Describe and give examples of generalizations and principles about what you recorded.

    c. Generate and defend inferences about what you recorded.

3. **Revising:** Students make substantive changes to their knowledge of the content, responding to prompts such as the following.

a. What are some things you now realize you were wrong about regarding what you recorded?

b. What are some things you now realize you should add to your notes about what you recorded?

c. What are some things you still don't understand or know about what you recorded?

This process is enhanced when using a proficiency scale. For example, when a teacher is about to introduce new knowledge, they can provide students with a proficiency scale containing related content they have already learned. The teacher asks students to record everything they remember about the previously learned measurement topic. The teacher then prompts students to add to what they recorded and answers questions that arise during the review. Finally, students revise what they wrote to reflect new learning they acquired during the activity.

Instructional Groups and Centers

In contrast to traditional education systems, where instruction usually takes place in a whole-group context, schools implementing competency-based practices typically deliver most instruction in small-group or individual contexts. Marzano, Aschoff, and Avila (2022) wrote the following about such schools:

> *Every class period will involve grouping students, except in situations when the teacher decides that all students require direct instruction on the same topic. . . . Another common convention is for the teacher to conduct whole-class instruction for a short time at the beginning, middle, or end of a class period. (p. 111)*

Thus, in classrooms using competency-based practices, whole-group instruction is used strategically or only when it is clear that the entire class needs instruction on a particular topic (Marzano et al., 2017). The teacher uses student data related to specific measurement topics to determine when each type of grouping is most appropriate.

Competency-based grouping practices involve bringing students together for very specific reasons. For example, students working on the same topic might be grouped for instruction on that topic. At a more granular level, students working on specific learning targets related to a topic might be grouped together. However, these groups *must be flexible*. If a student demonstrates proficiency with a particular topic or learning target, they will likely need to transition out of their current group and into either individual work or a different group focused on their next topic or learning target. According to Marzano and Abbott (2022), "Teachers should always keep in mind that grouping in a competency-based classroom should be flexible. Indeed, some groups might be established on a one-time basis and disband when the need has been met" (p. 86).

For example, imagine a teacher uses evidence from an assessment to create three groups, each receiving tailored support based on their specific needs. The first group consists of learners who exhibit errors of omission or misconceptions, indicating gaps in foundational knowledge or potential misunderstandings from incorrectly encoded information. These students benefit from targeted direct instruction to address critical missing elements and clarify misunderstandings. The second group is suited for guided instruction. These learners demonstrate a basic understanding but may have minor errors that can be corrected with guided reflection and attention to specific mistakes. Once they adjust these errors, they can further solidify their understanding or practice the skill to strengthen their grasp of the content. The third group, the independent practice group, is made up of learners who have demonstrated a strong grasp of the concept or skill. These students are ready for deeper learning experiences that enhance nuanced understanding and allow for more fluent, independent practice of the skill. This structured approach ensures each group receives the appropriate level of support to advance their learning effectively.

Teachers should keep in mind the fluid nature of competency-based instructional groups when designing the physical layout of the classroom. Marzano, Aschoff, and Avila (2022) elaborated on this idea:

> Forming and reforming groups requires movement, which can be facilitated or hindered by the organization of the classroom. Groups also need spaces to gather and work on activities. However, whole-class instruction will still occur.
>
> Consequently, teachers should ensure that they can easily monitor the entire class; that all students can easily hear and see the teacher and any whiteboard, flipchart, or other resource in use; and that there are walkways so students can access materials or leave to use the restroom. (p. 141)

Groups will also need clear roles and responsibilities to function effectively. Roles and responsibilities will vary depending on the purpose of the group. The following are examples.

- **Processing new knowledge:** Roles might include facilitator, summarizer, representor, and notetaker.
- **Practicing new knowledge:** Roles might include accuracy monitor, fluency timer, and coach.

- **Examining similarities and differences:** Roles might include comparer, classifier, metaphor maven, and analogy artist.
- **Engaging in complex tasks:** Roles might include decision maker, problem solver, investigator, inventor, and systems analyzer.

And, most importantly, groups need a disbanding strategy. As Marzano, Aschoff, and Avila (2022) explained, "Sometimes groups simply run their course and stop benefiting student learning" (p. 116). If a group reaches a point where their learning tasks are best done independently, it is time for that group to dissolve. The group can always reconvene later if circumstances indicate the need to do so.

If teachers are spending most of their instructional time working with small groups of students, effective centers are essential for providing support and learning opportunities to students who are not currently participating in a small group with the teacher. A *center* is an area of the classroom where students can refine skills or extend their understanding of information. Marzano, Aschoff, and Avila (2022) recommended planning for centers by looking at a proficiency scale that many students in the class are currently working on and asking the three following questions.

1. Is there new information related to this learning target that a center could help students learn?
2. What activities could the center include to help students deepen their understanding related to this learning target?
3. What activities could the center include to help students practice a skill related to this learning target?

Centers can involve online learning, hands-on practice, or pencil-and-paper activities. For example, teacher-created screencasts are excellent tools for centers. Teachers simply record a short video of themselves addressing the content in a specific proficiency scale that students can watch while they are at the center (Marzano & Abbott, 2022). Alternatively, if the teacher has screencasts of students demonstrating their understanding of a specific proficiency scale (generated during assessments as described in chapter 5, page 89), they could use these as the focus of a center. Creating their own screencasts could also serve as a center activity for students.

Blended Instruction

For a competency-based classroom to work, it must use blended instruction. *Blended instruction* integrates online instructional resources with instructional support from the teacher. According to Marzano and Hardy (2023), blended instruction "is an essential component" of competency-based classrooms, "not an optional one" (p. 106). For blended instruction to be effective, teachers must match online learning resources (such as videos, quizzes, and activities) to their measurement topics. Then, students can easily locate resources that they can use individually to learn more about specific learning targets they are working on.

Blended instruction is also an excellent tool to support students who are working on advanced topics or other enrichment activities. For example, when planning instructional units, teachers can create online activities and add them to an online class site or learning management system for students to access anytime, from anywhere. As students demonstrate proficiency and are ready for enrichment or advanced topics, the next activities are readily available to keep them motivated and engaged in their learning.

Additionally, teachers who are implementing competency-based practices in their classrooms may have access to e-learning platforms or intelligent tutoring systems. Researchers Leonard Tetzlaff, Florian Schmiedek, and Garvin Brod (2021) reported that such programs not only adjust the difficulty of subsequent learning tasks based on student performance on previous tasks, but also tailor instruction to learner's psychological states and learning preferences. Further, meta-analyses by educators Wenting Ma, Olusola O. Adesope, John C. Nesbit, and Qing Liu (2014) and researchers Saiying Steenbergen-Hu and Harris Cooper (2014) have found that such systems lead to increased student achievement across multiple subject areas and contexts. Therefore, if teachers have access to such programs and platforms, they can also plan to use these for independent student learning. However, a word of caution about such programs and platforms: Levine and Patrick (2019) warned that while such software "enables flexible pacing" it also "minimizes the role and richness of the teacher and the classroom environment" (p. 7). It should therefore be used as a single tool in a comprehensive tool kit from which teachers can select when planning various types of instruction for students.

Summary

When teachers implement competency-based practices related to instruction, focus shifts from direct instruction to students' interactions with the content. Teachers facilitate student learning through strategies such as chunking, which breaks information into manageable parts and helps students manage their working memory. Previewing, representing, and processing strategies help students manage their engagement and monitor their understanding of the information they are learning. The context of learning is also influenced by competency-based practices, as instructional groups and centers take center stage in the classroom, supplemented and enhanced by blended instruction. These instructional strategies and design principles, like the competency-based practices associated with the other domains, empower students to take ownership of their learning while ensuring effective teacher guidance in a collaborative and adaptive environment.

CHAPTER 7

Adult Roles

Almost all competency-based practices presuppose that the adults in a school—teachers, administrators, counselors, support staff, and others—adjust their interactions with students; educators take on new roles and let go of traditional roles. For example, a teacher's role shifts from largely instructional to mostly facilitative (McPherson, 2021; Sutherland & Strunk, 2021). As Marzano and Abbott (2022) explained, implementation of competency-based practices "ultimately changes the role of the teacher" toward being "a facilitator of learning, as opposed to solely an instructor of content" (p. 151).

While this shift in adult roles can eventually be fulfilling and enjoyable for educators, many initially struggle with re-envisioning the dynamics of their interactions with students. Researchers Christopher Prokes, Patrick R. Lowenthal, Chareen Snelson, and Kerry Rice (2021) found that implementation of competency-based practices is often criticized because it forces teachers to "move from traditional content experts to become mentors or guides" (p. 2). Journalist Paul Fain (2014) and educator Nicki Monahan (2015) both observed struggles among educators as they adapted to their new roles.

In our experience implementing competency-based structures and practices, we have observed at least two types of teachers who seem to have the most difficulty in transitioning to competency-based practices. First, there are highly effective teachers who have independently created a thriving traditional classroom where students frequently achieve desired educational outcomes. If these teachers do not receive adequate support during the implementation of competency-based practices, they may feel devalued and vulnerable, as their self-perception of success would now depend, at least in part, on the actions of others.

Second, there are some traditional classroom teachers who have plateaued in their desire to implement new and more effective pedagogical practices. These teachers sometimes resist seeking help and support for fear of being labeled ineffective. These teachers are often able to overcome their hesitancy once they realize they are not alone, have access to supportive coaching, and will be granted a grace period by school leadership as they realign and reinvigorate their pedagogical practices.

These concerns and worries among teachers should not be underestimated. Fortunately, with the right guidance, they can be addressed, allowing teachers to see themselves not as isolated in their efforts but as part of an effective pedagogical team working together for better outcomes for all students. McPherson (2021) found that the experiences of teachers and principals who persisted with their implementation of competency-based practices ultimately found their new roles "worthwhile" and "successful" (p. 10). Additionally, collaboration during the implementation of competency-based practices can help reduce a teacher's personal workload. Marzano and colleagues (2017) noted that moving toward a system of competency-based practices "can reduce the difficulty of in-classroom work for teachers and enhance the learning experience of students," and that many teachers say that once they get used to competency-based practices, "they find the teaching process much more rewarding" (p. 70).

Educator Catherine K. Toland (2017) found that adult roles beyond the teacher need to shift too. According to McPherson (2021), these shifts require educators to take responsibility for "targeted professional development, restructuring of school and class schedules to accommodate collaboration, cooperative vertical mapping strategies, and redesigned preservice training for new teachers" (p. 3). In sum, competency-based practices necessitate a shift in adult roles; when managed well, this shift can ultimately result in greater satisfaction and fulfillment for adults in the school's learning community.

There are five questions that guide a school's decision making relative to adult roles.

1. How will we manage student groupings, including initial placements and midyear moves?
2. How will we manage scheduling?
3. How will we manage teacher-student relationships to prevent students from getting lost in the shuffle?

4. How will we manage pacing and ensure that students do not lag behind the pace needed for on-time graduation?

5. How will we ensure continued professional learning for adults in the school?

Possibly the most important role of adults related to implementing competency-based practices is grouping students into classes. And, since "student grouping is intimately tied to scheduling" (Marzano et al., 2017, p. 69), scheduling is also a critical adult role. We begin this chapter by addressing these two crucial topics, before discussing teacher-student relationships, pacing, and professional learning.

Student Groupings

A flagship competency-based practice is the idea that students do not move to the next level of content in a specific subject area until they have demonstrated proficiency at the level they are currently working on. Conversely, once a student has demonstrated proficiency at the level they are currently working on for a specific subject area, they move to the next level, regardless of their age or whether it is the beginning, middle, or end of the school year. This practice has great potential in terms of amplifying the efficiency of classroom instruction and building on students' interests. As Marzano and colleagues (2017) observed, when students are grouped by age, teachers "must differentiate curriculum, instruction, and assessment for a wide range of students" (p. 133). But when students are grouped by proficiency, "a teacher is dealing with either only one level of student competence or a few relatively well-defined levels of competence" (Marzano et al., 2017, p. 133). However, creating a system that allows this approach to function productively in practice can be challenging.

First, such a system requires a high level of transparency and communication among students, teachers, administrators, and parents or guardians. As Marzano and Kosena (2022) explained, "Since most schools operate under a grade-leveled, single-classroom assignment model, some students and parents might be wary of a midyear move" (p. 156).

Second, such a system must consider other factors besides proficiency, such as teacher-student relationships, a student's peer relationships, preserving age-appropriate social groups, and so on. Again, Marzano and Kosena (2022) cautioned that "student-teacher relationships matter, as do the social dynamics among students" (pp. 156–157). Anecdotally, we have heard from students who graduated from competency-based systems that midyear moves to a different class with a different teacher could be disappointing, especially if the student had a strong attachment to the teacher whose class they were leaving.

Third, depending on the format of required state tests (which are typically incongruent with competency-based class groupings), parents and students need to understand that it may be necessary to regroup students by age to complete the tests to comply with state administration rules.

Finally, such a system must ensure that all stakeholders understand the reasons for student groupings, the goals that each student is striving to meet, the action steps that students can take to meet their goals, and the strategies that the adults in the school are using to support students toward their goals. Parents or guardians should understand and have evidence that facilitates their trust that groupings are designed to provide what students need, not to punish or reward them for their school performance. Again, Marzano and Kosena (2022) explained the matter further:

> Switching a student's classroom might cause concern with some parents or guardians in that they might interpret such a change as evidence their child is failing or something is wrong regarding the child's progress. This renders the school's communication with the student and his or her family critical. (p. 157)

In sum, a system that facilitates student groupings by proficiency instead of age, when designed and implemented well, forms an essential foundation for other competency-based practices. Additionally, a system that presupposes student movement in the middle of the school year (based on growth and demonstration of proficiency) can take the pressure off initial placements for incoming students, whether they are new to the school or just entering the school system (as with preschoolers and kindergartners). But such a system must be designed, run, and monitored carefully to prevent serious issues from arising or escalating.

In the absence of any preexisting data about a student, the simplest way to make an initial placement is by the student's age (Marzano et al., 2017). In Westminster Public Schools, initial placements include a two- to three-week observation period during which teachers assess the new student's skills and knowledge. Classroom placements are adjusted if necessary to ensure students receive the appropriate instruction and support (Gotto et al., 2025).

However, the absence of any preexisting data about a student is hopefully a rare occurrence. Because of its relative consistency and availability, state-level assessment data can be used as a better starting point for initial placement. That is, if a student scored at the proficient level on a state test, they are placed according to their age for that subject area. If they scored below or above proficient, they are placed in a lower or higher level, respectively, than their age would suggest (Marzano et al., 2017).

Whether educators use age or state-testing data for initial placements, these data must be used as a *starting point only*. There is no necessary link between age and proficiency; Marzano and Kosena (2022) pointed out "not all eight-year-old students have the same reading or mathematical ability just because they are eight years old" (p. 156). And most large-scale assessments are designed to provide trend data about *groups* of students rather than specific feedback about individual student performance on discrete learning targets (Marzano et al., 2019). To improve the accuracy of initial placements, schools might add data from district or school placement tests (Marzano et al., 2017). If designed well, placement tests can give more specific data about individual competence for the learning targets at certain levels of a subject area.

As mentioned previously, communication is critical to any system of student grouping. One important point of communication about initial placements is how they differ from traditional systems where students are placed into "tracks" for particular content areas or retained because they did not perform well enough at a particular grade level. Marzano and colleagues (2017) explained how competency-based grouping practices are different from traditional tracking and retention practices:

> In a traditional system, an elementary student would be held back if he or she did not receive a passing grade in a majority of the content areas at a particular grade level. That student would have to take all content areas over again, even the parts in which he or she had already demonstrated proficiency. In high school, if a student does not pass a course, he or she must take the entire course over—even the parts he or she already knows. In a CBE system, students only need to work on the material on which they have not yet demonstrated proficiency. (p. 135)

To conclude this section, we will emphasize again the most essential element of any competency-based grouping system: flexibility. To illustrate the importance of flexibility, consider the following two scenarios.

1. Suppose a new student in a school is placed into grade 6 mathematics. After three weeks of instruction, the teacher has seen enough evidence from assessments and discussions with the student to demonstrate that he has been misplaced and actually needs to move up to grade 7 mathematics. The teacher requests a meeting with the school-level grouping committee (administrator, grade 7 mathematics teacher, instructional coach, school psychologist, and an intervention staff member) to discuss the placement. The team agrees with the teacher that the student should move up to grade 7 mathematics, notifies the student's parents of the planned transition to grade 7 mathematics, and moves the student to his new class grouping for mathematics as soon as possible (Marzano & Abbott, 2022).

2. Suppose a student has mastered all the learning targets for grade 8 mathematics and is ready to progress to grade 9 content. Depending

on the school and district policies, grade 9 mathematics could be credit bearing, part of a student's graduation requirements, and taught only by teachers at the high school building. If the student is currently attending a middle school building (and working at the middle school level in other subject areas), educators may need to collaborate and develop policies and procedures to ensure that the student receives high school credit for working on grade 9 mathematics, even if they are not attending the high school building where it is typically taught. Districts must create ways for teachers to promote acceleration for students who are ready, even if that means collaborating across buildings.

According to Marzano, Aschoff, and Avila (2022), this flexibility and movement between groupings is the "essence" of a competency-based system: "Once students demonstrate competence relative to a specific topic, they are not required to experience further instruction relative to that topic" (p. 115).

Scheduling

Second only to their grouping responsibilities, adults in schools implementing competency-based practices have a responsibility to create a schedule that allows students to access instruction at the specific level they are working at for each subject area without missing out on any instruction that they also need for other subject areas. As Marzano and Kosena (2022) stated, this adult role requires educators in a school to adopt a "highly flexible schedule" (p. 156). There are several ways to achieve a highly flexible schedule, but the commonality among all approaches is that the schedule "must allow students to receive instruction from multiple teachers throughout the school day" (Marzano & Kosena, 2022, p. 153).

The goal of competency-based scheduling practices is "for students to receive instruction, support, and feedback in each subject area on content that is appropriate to their current level of development" (Marzano & Hardy, 2023, p. 36). Scheduling approaches fall on a continuum ranging from approaches that are less disruptive to traditional schedules, such as focused instruction time, to approaches that completely rethink scheduling, such as collective strengths-based teaching. Figure 7.1 depicts this continuum.

Focused instruction time	Organization around competencies	Content-area saturation	Collective strengths-based teaching
●	●	●	●

Figure 7.1: Continuum of competency-based scheduling approaches.

As Marzano and colleagues (2017) stated, "There is no single best way to create a CBE schedule" (p. 133). You will need to decide which scheduling approach is most appropriate for your school. Here, we briefly describe each approach shown in figure 7.1.

Focused Instruction Time

Focused instruction time (FIT) simply adds an extra period to the school day during which students receive whatever instruction they need most. In secondary schools with defined class and lunch periods, shaving just five minutes off each existing period in a day can yield enough time for a daily thirty-to-forty-minute FIT period. In elementary schools, these periods might be incorporated into a lunch rotation, as shown in figure 7.2.

Block	Monday	Tuesday	Wednesday	Thursday	Friday
8:15 a.m.	Homeroom	Homeroom	Homeroom	Homeroom	Homeroom
8:30 a.m.	English language arts	English language arts and spelling	English language arts	English language arts and spelling	Independent work on projects
9:00 a.m.	English language arts				
9:30 a.m.	Literacy or reading				
10:00 a.m.	Physical education	Music	Social studies	Physical education	Art
10:30 a.m.	Mathematics				
11:30 a.m.	A lunch B FIT time	A lunch B FIT time	A lunch B FIT time	A lunch B FIT time	A lunch B FIT time
Noon	A FIT time B lunch	A FIT time B lunch	A FIT time B lunch	A FIT time B lunch	A FIT time B lunch
12:30 p.m.	Science				
1:00 p.m.	Science	Health	Science	Media	Media
1:30 p.m.	Social studies	Physical education	Physical education	Social studies	Physical education
2:00 p.m.	English language arts	English language arts	Mathematics	English language arts	Mathematics
2:30 p.m.	Dismissal				

Source: Adapted from Marzano et al., 2017.
Figure 7.2: Focused instruction time as part of a lunch rotation.

During these FIT periods, students have full access to all teachers. Depending on their current instructional needs and goals, each student goes to the appropriate classroom or teacher for support. Marzano and colleagues (2017) described FIT as "a structured study hall based on students' needs" (p. 138), and Marzano and Kosena (2022) pointed out the following:

> The possibilities of a FIT block are vast, but the results are the same: every student is provided a dedicated block of time every day to receive targeted, personalized instruction that does not interfere with or take away from his or her access to the direct instruction of the day's lesson plan. (p. 155)

As Marzano and Hardy (2023) described, FIT blocks might also be used for tutorial time, free exploration of personally interesting topics, and enrichment opportunities.

Importantly, Marzano and Hardy (2023) suggested a variation of FIT for the high school level. This manifestation is called *content-area bullpens*, in reference to the baseball practice of keeping a pitcher warmed up and ready to be used at any time:

> In a high school, different teachers would be scheduled in their content-area bullpen at different times. In a large comprehensive high school, then, there would be one or more mathematics teachers in the mathematics bullpen during every period. Consequently, students know that they can go to the mathematics bullpen at any time and there will be someone there to help them with whatever mathematics topics they need support on. (p. 37)

In sum, FIT offers a flexible scheduling option to ensure that students receive the targeted support they need in a dedicated time slot each day, ultimately enhancing their learning experience without detracting from regular lesson plans.

Organization Around Competencies

A school schedule design that is slightly more disruptive to traditional schedules than FIT has all students at all levels focus on a specific subject area during the same period of the school day. Critically, this approach assumes that teachers are qualified to teach multiple subject areas and, therefore, usually works best at the elementary and—in some cases—middle school levels. Figure 7.3 illustrates how to construct this type of schedule.

The advantage of this kind of schedule is that it increases flexibility in regrouping students (Marzano et al., 2017). If a student is initially placed in the wrong level for a specific content area, they simply transition to a different level of that content area, which is taught during the same time period as the level they were in initially.

	Period 1	Period 2	Period 3	Lunch/Recess	Period 4	Period 5
Teacher A	ELA	Mathematics	Science		Social Studies	Electives
Teacher B	ELA	Mathematics	Science		Social Studies	Electives
Teacher C	ELA	Mathematics	Science		Social Studies	Electives
Teacher D	ELA	Mathematics	Science		Social Studies	Electives
Teacher E	ELA	Mathematics	Science		Social Studies	Electives
Teacher F	ELA	Mathematics	Science		Social Studies	Electives
Teacher G	ELA	Mathematics	Science		Social Studies	Electives
Teacher H	ELA	Mathematics	Science		Social Studies	Electives
Teacher I	ELA	Mathematics	Science		Social Studies	Electives
Teacher J	ELA	Mathematics	Science		Social Studies	Electives
Teacher K	ELA	Mathematics	Science		Social Studies	Electives
Teacher L	ELA	Mathematics	Science		Social Studies	Electives
Teacher M	ELA	Mathematics	Science		Social Studies	Electives
Teacher N	ELA	Mathematics	Science		Social Studies	Electives
Teacher O	ELA	Mathematics	Science		Social Studies	Electives

Source: Finn & Finn, 2021, p. 53.
Figure 7.3: Organization around competencies.

However, especially at the secondary level, there may be significant challenges to implementing this type of schedule. As aforementioned, teachers are generally specialists at the secondary level. Therefore, secondary scheduling might take an approach more focused on content-area saturation, as described next.

Content-Area Saturation

This approach might be seen as the converse of organization around competencies. As figure 7.4 (page 140) shows, content-area saturation involves offering multiple levels of the same subject area during a period of the school day (Marzano & Hardy, 2023).

This gives the teachers options in terms of differentiation for the students assigned to their subject area for that period; they might exchange students based on personalized needs and goals or combine classes to free up one teacher to provide small-group or one-to-one intervention or acceleration. From the students' perspective, this prevents the need for schedule overhauls when a student transitions from one level to the next level for a specific subject area. While content-area saturation's requirement for multiple levels of the same subject area can strain a school's master schedule, it can be a productive option for secondary schools implementing competency-based practices.

	Period 1	Period 2	Period 3	Lunch/Recess	Period 4	Period 5
Teacher A	ELA	ELA	ELA		ELA	ELA
Teacher B	ELA	ELA	ELA		ELA	ELA
Teacher C	ELA	ELA	ELA		ELA	ELA
Teacher D	Mathematics	Mathematics	Mathematics		Mathematics	Mathematics
Teacher E	Mathematics	Mathematics	Mathematics		Mathematics	Mathematics
Teacher F	Mathematics	Mathematics	Mathematics		Mathematics	Mathematics
Teacher G	Science	Science	Science		Science	Science
Teacher H	Science	Science	Science		Science	Science
Teacher I	Science	Science	Science		Science	Science
Teacher J	Social Studies	Social Studies	Social Studies		Social Studies	Social Studies
Teacher K	Social Studies	Social Studies	Social Studies		Social Studies	Social Studies
Teacher L	Social Studies	Social Studies	Social Studies		Social Studies	Social Studies
Teacher M	Electives	Electives	Electives		Electives	Electives
Teacher N	Electives	Electives	Electives		Electives	Electives
Teacher O	Electives	Electives	Electives		Electives	Electives

Source: Finn & Finn, 2021, p. 53.
Figure 7.4: Content-area saturation.

Collective Strengths-Based Teaching

Possibly the most radical approach to accommodate competency-based practices through scheduling is what Marzano and Kosena (2022) called a *collective teaching approach*. In this approach, the school leader identifies those teachers who are best at whole-class direct instruction, small-group facilitation and coaching, and individualized, one-to-one tutoring. Then the school leader does the following:

> Designs a flexible schedule that assigns some teachers to direct instruction of large groups of students, while other teachers conduct small-group instruction, and still others preside over individualized instruction. Teachers are assigned to topics not only based on their knowledge of the topics, but also based on their expertise at teaching large groups, small groups, and individuals. (Marzano & Kosena, 2022, pp. 153–154)

In this approach, students are assigned to sessions based on their content-area needs, and also their need for whole-group, small-group, or individualized instruction. Notably, this approach is certainly not a good fit for all schools; parameters related to school norms and collective bargaining agreements may preclude it from consideration. However, for those schools that can make it work, it offers yet another approach to competency-based scheduling.

In closing this section, we encourage you to think outside of the confines of traditional scheduling constraints and obstacles when thinking about implementing competency-based practices. For example, students might not be able to engage in one-to-one tutoring before or after school, but could you offer one-to-one tutoring sessions for specific subjects during lunch periods, inviting students to eat and learn at the same time? For students who can't attend Saturday school or summer school programs, could you offer targeted recovery programs online, focused on a subset of measurement topics at a specific level or levels for which many students need additional support? Implementing competency-based scheduling requires educators to creatively navigate traditional constraints to meet the diverse instructional needs of their students. By exploring flexible scheduling approaches such as FIT, organization around competencies, content-area saturation, and collective strengths-based teaching, schools can better align instruction with individual student levels, ultimately fostering a more effective and responsive learning environment.

Teacher-Student Relationships

As adults in schools implementing competency-based practices design grouping and scheduling systems to support student growth in specific levels of specific subject areas, it is frequently a concern that students will get lost in the shuffle. In other words, educators and parents worry students will suffer because they lack strong yearlong relationships with specific homeroom or grade-level teachers. It is the responsibility of adults in a school implementing competency-based practices to ensure that students have the relational support that they need for success while also providing the targeted instructional support they require to achieve proficiency at their current level. To this end, setting up an advisory system can be an excellent option to manage student-teacher relationships in a system of competency-based practices.

While most often used at the secondary level, advisory systems can also be successful in an elementary school. At its core, an advisory system assigns each student to a specific adult in the building who is responsible for at least the following four things (Marzano et al., 2017).

1. Knowing the student's background, interests, and challenges
2. Receiving all information related to the student
3. Being available to the student
4. Acting as an advocate for the student

The adult adviser will certainly not be able to provide instructional support in all (or possibly any) of the areas where the student may need content assistance. However, that is not the adviser's role. Instead, the adviser helps students identify which areas they need support in, which adults in the building can provide that support, and when and how to appropriately access that support. Advisers can also discuss students' life goals or nonacademic concerns.

Teachers also benefit from an advisory system. If a teacher has questions about a particular student, they can start by asking the student's adviser. For example, at Westminster High School, each student is assigned to an academic enrichment teacher who functions much like an adviser. Academic enrichment teachers follow the same group of students throughout their entire high school career; the academic enrichment teachers are the ones who call out their students' names when they walk across the stage during graduation. In addition to providing mentorship and advisement to students, academic enrichment classes also involve team-building and relationship-building activities. In the parlance of the Westminster High School community, academic enrichment classes are like "homeroom on steroids" and help "keep a big school small."

Pacing

Closely related to grouping and scheduling is another important adult role in competency-based systems: monitoring student pace and ensuring that students do not lag behind the pace needed for on-time graduation. To begin our discussion of pacing, let's address a few misconceptions about competency-based practices related to pacing. Competency-based pacing is neither "a single learning pathway that students simply navigate at different speeds" (Levine & Patrick, 2019, p. 5) nor, according to educators Eljim P. Cuyacot and Marilo T. Cuyacot (2022), a way in which "students can keep working at the same learning target for as long as they want" (p. 96).

Competency-based pacing means that adults in the school intervene with students to ensure that they achieve mastery of each learning target in a time frame that ensures they will graduate on time. According to Levine and Patrick (2019), "Schools [are] actively monitoring progress and providing more instruction and support if students are not on a trajectory to graduate by age 18 or soon after" (p. 5). Thus, monitoring pace—and intervening to speed up pace when necessary—also constitutes an important adult role in schools implementing competency-based practices.

That said, it's also one of the most difficult adult roles in schools implementing competency-based practices. Researchers Gabriel Reif, Greta Shultz, and Steven Ellis (2016) identified pacing as a prime candidate for innovation in the competency-based practices space and a factor that severely limits competency-based practice implementation, especially at the high school level. Evans and colleagues (2019) found that pacing is a primary area where school leaders need to direct resources and support. Fortunately, they also found that building a comprehensive assessment system—such as we described in chapter 5 (page 89)—can go far toward alleviating issues with measuring pace.

Once such an assessment system is in place, summative scores can be used to create a pace metric. As with scheduling, there is no single best way to report pace (Marzano et al., 2017). However, there are some logical guidelines that can be used to create pacing scores. Marzano and Abbott (2022) explained one such approach:

> *One popular CBE metric is to report how many of the proficiency scales at a given grade level and subject area the student has mastered. For example, assume that there are twenty proficiency scales for fifth-grade mathematics. If a student has reached proficiency (that is, demonstrated competence at the score 3.0 level) for ten of these scales, the student's status would be represented as the simple ratio 10/20. (p. 152)*

This ratio can then be used to determine whether a student is on pace, ahead of pace, or behind pace for a specific grade or level. Marzano and Abbott (2022) continued:

> *The most straightforward way to report pace is to divide the school year into equal units based on the number of proficiency scales students must complete within a year. Again using fifth-grade mathematics as an example, students must complete the twenty proficiency scales by the end of the school year, which is thirty-six weeks in length. To accomplish this, students should complete a proficiency scale once every 1.8 weeks (that is, 36 ÷ 20 = 1.8). Assume that after eighteen weeks of the school year, a particular student has completed ten proficiency scales. That student would be considered on pace, whereas a student who had completed eight proficiency scales would be considered behind pace, and a student who had completed twelve proficiency scales would be considered ahead of pace. (p. 152)*

This model must be used with caution, as not all proficiency scales are equal; some may require four weeks to demonstrate proficiency, while others may take only one. School teams must carefully monitor the accuracy of the "on pace," "behind pace," and "ahead of pace" indicators and adjust where necessary.

As highlighted in chapter 1 (page 25), a system that has implemented competency-based practices requiring each student to demonstrate proficiency on each measurement topic for each level of each subject area before moving on to the next level makes it impossible to report overall or omnibus grades for students. Instead, such a system might report a student's status for their current level—how many of the proficiency scales they have mastered so far—along with their status for each previous level—always at least 3.0 (Proficient), but 4.0 (Advanced) if they achieved that score on the majority of topics at that level—for each subject area, as shown in figure 7.5 (page 144).

Level	Art	Career Literacy	Mathematics	Personal and Social Skills	English Language Arts	Science	Social Studies	Technology
Advanced (3)	▓			▓			▓	▓
Advanced (2)								
Advanced (1)								
10	▓			▓				▓
09	▓			▓				▓
08	▓			▓				▓
07	▓							
06								
05								
04		2 of 16	21 of 35	4 of 6	3 of 36	17 of 25		
03	9 of 10	3.0 (Proficient)	3.0 (Proficient)		4.0 (Advanced)	3.0 (Proficient)	13 of 15	7 of 8
02	3.0 (Proficient)	3.0 (Proficient)	4.0 (Advanced)	3.0 (Proficient)	3.0 (Proficient)	3.0 (Proficient)	3.0 (Proficient)	4.0 (Advanced)
01	3.0 (Proficient)	3.0 (Proficient)	4.0 (Advanced)	3.0 (Proficient)	3.0 (Proficient)	3.0 (Proficient)	3.0 (Proficient)	3.0 (Proficient)

Note: The darker shaded cells indicate levels that do not apply to the subject area.

Source: Marzano et al., 2017, p. 156.

Figure 7.5: Reporting student status for current and previous levels.

Following this approach one step further, information such as that shown in figure 7.5 can be used to report a student's overall pace. For example, look at the mathematics column of figure 7.5. Of the thirteen levels, the student has completed three of the levels and has completed twenty-one of the thirty-five topics for their current level. Instead of saying that this student is earning an A, B, or C in mathematics (which is almost meaningless in systems requiring mastery at one level before moving on to the next), you might report that this student is at level 3.6 in mathematics. That is, they have completed three levels and are 60 percent (or 0.6) of the way through level 4. Such a pace metric, when paired with a student's age, can be compared to data representing appropriate progress toward on-time graduation by age eighteen. If such a comparison reveals that a student is behind pace, interventions should be implemented to help the student return to an appropriate pace.

Professional Learning

Adults in schools implementing competency-based practices are busy folks. They have critical responsibilities, such as grouping, scheduling, advising, and pacing, without which the system cannot be maintained. In the busy life of an educator implementing competency-based practices, it is easy to forget that the adults in the school have a responsibility to continue their own learning. Competency-based practices are not always intuitive, especially those that run counter to traditional models of schooling. Additionally, adults in schools may have to learn additional skills to effectively lead the implementation of competency-based practices, such as systems thinking, change management, and conflict resolution. Educators implementing competency-based practices must not neglect their own professional learning and growth. In fact, educators' professional learning is a critical element of implementing competency-based practices, as McPherson (2021) found in his study of student-centered learning: "Throughout the study, a recurring, unconventional theme emerged of the teacher and principal assuming the role of a learner" (p. 9).

Unfortunately, research shows that the professional learning and growth of adults in competency-based systems are often neglected. Researchers Andrew P. Kelly and Rooney Columbus (2016) evaluated 380 studies of competency-based practice implementation and found few references to training and professional development focused on competency-based practices. Educators Diana Gilmer Echols, Patricia W. Neely, and Diane Dusick (2018) surveyed seventy teachers implementing competency-based practices and noted that professional learning and continued training around competency-based practices were needed; they also suggested that such training could productively be provided using a competency-based model. For example, Sutherland and Strunk (2021) stated that instructional coaching should be one of the primary methods of providing professional learning and support to teachers and other educators implementing competency-based practices. Specifically, they recommended that instructional coaching for competency-based practices be mandatory for all implementing educators and that educators be provided with release time to engage in such coaching:

> While some CBE districts have invested significant resources in an instructional coaching model, these resources are largely going underutilized. To improve implementation efforts, districts need to do more than invest in and mandate instructional coaching. Instead, districts should provide release time for teachers to participate. (Sutherland & Strunk, 2021, p. 17)

To guide instructional coaching, schools can develop measurement topics and proficiency scales for teachers. In the same way that students set goals and work toward them, teachers (with support from their instructional coach) can set goals and work toward them. For example, a school or district can develop proficiency scales for each component of its instructional model. Teachers can then set goals based on the model and receive job-embedded professional development and instructional coaching that aligns with the model and supports their specific goals; we presented one such approach for this type of job-embedded professional learning in chapter 4—instructional rounds. Additionally, Sutherland and Strunk (2021) suggested the following:

> Instructional coaching, professional development sessions, and professional learning communities could provide teachers opportunities to engage in discussions that unpack and challenge their practice's professional norms, giving teachers a space to discuss and reflect on their changing role in a CBE system. (p. 18)

Such an approach to professional learning can go a long way toward creating a safe space for teachers to innovate and try out different facets of competency-based practices. As Marzano and Hardy (2023) stated, "Leaders should remind teachers that they are not expected to perfectly employ CBE from the outset. The school leader should create safe space for the educators implementing CBE to fail and then learn from their failures" (p. 87). If teachers set goals and then track their progress toward those goals, it creates a system in which they can attempt innovations, their failures can be acknowledged and corrected, and their continuous improvement is celebrated and reinforced.

Summary

When schools implement competency-based practices, adult roles change. As teachers transition from direct instruction to more student-centered approaches, other adults in the school must also transform their thinking about their roles. Educators responsible for student grouping and scheduling will need to engage in careful planning and clear communication to ensure that students progress based on their proficiency, learning at a pace appropriate for an on-time graduation. Adults must also ensure that relationships are not sacrificed as competency-based practices are implemented; whether through an advisory, homeroom, or other system, adults are responsible for making sure that no student is overlooked by the system. To make these shifts, educators will need to prioritize their own professional development and learning, cultivating new mindsets and ways of thinking about school and student learning. This type of environment, where both students and adults are learning and growing, is excellent soil for competency-based practices to take root and flourish.

Epilogue

The transition to competency-based education is not an easy one. In fact, in his study of teacher and principal perceptions of implementing competency-based practices, McPherson (2021) specifically warned educators who are seeking to make the transition that it will involve "philosophical angst" and "change consequences" (p. 10). Bingham and colleagues (2021) reported that implementing competency-based practices brings many of the same implementation issues that plague other educational innovations: inconsistency, misalignment, unclear expectations, and lack of capacity. Evans and colleagues (2019) articulated the following list of implementation challenges based on their analysis of case studies from competency-based practice implementation in Maine schools and districts.

- Confusion about definitions and the focus of reform efforts
- Need to build parent and community knowledge about and support for the initiatives
- Lack of time for teachers to learn about and collaborate around competency-based practices
- Insufficient or misaligned funding
- Challenges surrounding selection and implementation of a learning management system and related technology
- Philosophical hurdles to changing grading and reporting processes and procedures

And these challenges don't go away after implementation is established. In their examination of a school that implemented competency-based practices over a decade prior to the study, Bingham and colleagues (2021) found that the school and its teachers were still addressing some of the same challenges that they had to overcome during implementation. Giving up too early also seems to be a hurdle that schools and districts struggle to overcome. Evans and colleagues (2020) warned against expecting to see immediate enhancement of student achievement outcomes: "Significant time is required to ensure [competency-based] practices are implemented to their full potential. . . . Collecting data on student outcomes too early could produce misleading results" (p. 17).

In our experience, successful implementation of competency-based practices is a recurring cycle of learning, implementing, reviewing, and revising. In fact, when Surr and colleagues (2022) examined competency-based practice implementations across the United States, they found that the most successful districts were those that "have come to recognize that deep transformation requires a sustained, multi-year commitment to change efforts" (p. 17). As new staff join a school or district, they will need their colleagues to help them understand how the competency-based practices in the system work together to accomplish the school's vision. In almost every way, implementing competency-based practices involves making a commitment to continuous monitoring and improvement over extended periods of time.

Encouragingly, it is possible to turn implementation barriers into implementation facilitators; those factors that often cause problems during implementation can simultaneously ease implementation. As an example, Evans and colleagues (2020) found that in some studies, lack of common definitions and expectations was a barrier to implementation, but in other studies, the presence of common definitions and expectations greatly facilitated implementation processes. The key to turning barriers into facilitators seems to have to do with what Evans and colleagues (2020) called the three *R*s of school-level change: (1) relevance, (2) readiness, and (3) resources, explained as follows.

- **Relevance:** Is the change relevant to the organization and its people?
- **Readiness:** Are the organization and its people ready for the change?
- **Resources:** Do the organization and its people have the resources necessary for the change?

Evans and colleagues (2020) explained that organizations who pay attention to the three *R*s are far more likely to experience factors such as alignment, communication, capacity, mindsets, sustainability, and technology as facilitators rather than barriers during implementation.

In this book, we have provided a series of questions that are designed to help you make decisions about your implementation of competency-based practices based, in many ways, on your school's specific profile relative to the three Rs. For example, the way you decide to make structure and reporting changes, as detailed in chapter 1 (page 25), will vary based how familiar your teachers are with competency-based instructional and grading practices (readiness). As described in chapter 2 (page 39), the student outcomes you decide to emphasize may vary based on what is most relevant to your student population (relevance). The level to which you explicitly teach agency and equity—as discussed in chapters 3 (page 59) and 4 (page 75)—will likely depend on the resources your school has available, both curricular and personnel (resources). Changes to assessment and instruction systems, as outlined in chapters 5 (page 89) and 6 (page 109), will need to align with both teachers' readiness to implement them and the resources available to support implementation (readiness and resources). And the way you choose to structure and maintain adult roles in your school, covered in chapter 7 (page 131), will need to be sensitive to what your students most need and what is most relevant to their current needs and goals (relevance).

As you embark on the journey toward implementing competency-based practices, or as you recommit to these transformational changes, our best hope is that you will do it thoughtfully. As Gagnon (2023) stated so eloquently, "Just as each learner is unique, there is no one right way to jump into competency-based education" (p. 10). Education is not a simple business, and improving outcomes for students always begins with logical, explainable, and sustainable decisions and commitments to systems, processes, and practices that will ensure each student masters the essential content of the curriculum. We wish you well and thank you for your commitment to innovation.

References

Abbott, D. M., Pelc, N., & Mercier, C. (2019). Cultural humility and the teaching of psychology. *Scholarship of Teaching and Learning in Psychology, 5*(2), 169–181. https://doi.org/10.1037/stl0000144

Ainscow, M. (2020). Promoting inclusion and equity in education: Lessons from international experiences. *Nordic Journal of Studies in Educational Policy, 6*(1), 7–16. https://doi.org/10.1080/20020317.2020.1729587

Alexander, K. L., Entwisle, D. R., & Olson, L. S. (2007). Lasting consequences of the summer learning gap. *American Sociological Review, 72*(2), 167–180. https://doi.org/10.1177/000312240707200202

ALSDE Special Education Services. (n.d.). *ALSDE proficiency scales.* Accessed at www.livebinders.com/b/3172074&present=true on February 16, 2025.

Anderson, S. A. (1994). *Synthesis of research on mastery learning.* Accessed at https://files.eric.ed.gov/fulltext/ED382567.pdf on December 12, 2024.

Arellanes, J. A., & Hendricks, M. (2022). Teaching ethnic-specific coursework: Practical suggestions for promoting diversity, equity, and inclusion within the classroom. *Teaching of Psychology, 49*(4), 369–375. https://doi.org/10.1177/00986283211013050

Arrowsmith, H. E., Houchens, G. W., Crossbourne-Richards, T.-A., Redifer, J. L., Zhang, J., & Norman, A. D. (2021). Operationalizing and measuring personalized learning in K–12 schools: Development and implementation of an innovation configuration map. *International Journal of Education Policy and Leadership, 17*(3), 1–16. https://doi.org/10.22230/ijepl.2021v17n3a977

Bill & Melinda Gates Foundation, Afton Partners, Eli & Edythe Broad Foundation, CEE Trust, Christensen Institute, Charter School Growth Fund, et al. (2014). *A working definition of personalized learning*. Bill & Melinda Gates Foundation. Accessed at https://assets.documentcloud.org/documents/1311874/personalized-learning-working-definition-fall2014.pdf on December 12, 2024.

Bingham, A. J., Adams, M., & Stewart, R. L. (2021). Competency-based education: Examining educators' experiences. *The Qualitative Report, 26*(3), 674–695. https://doi.org/10.46743/2160-3715/2021.4383

Blankenberger, B., Kerr, R., & Dooley, T. (2023). Competency based education pilot in Illinois: Preliminary findings. *Educational Policy, 38*(5), 1229–1256. https://doi.org/10.1177/08959048231198819

Block, J. H. (1978). The "C" in CBE. *Educational Researcher, 7*(5), 13–16. https://doi.org/10.3102/0013189X007005013

Block, J. H. (1979). Mastery learning: The current state of the craft. *Educational Leadership, 37*(2), 114–117. Accessed at https://ascd.org/el/articles/mastery-learning-the-current-state-of-the-craft on March 16, 2025.

Block, J. H., & Anderson, L. W. (1975). *Mastery learning in classroom instruction*. Macmillan.

Block, J. H., & Burns, R. B. (1976). Mastery learning. *Review of Research in Education, 4*(1), 3–49. https://doi.org/10.3102/0091732X004001003

Bloom, B. S. (Ed.). (1956). *Taxonomy of educational objectives: The classification of educational goals—Handbook 1. Cognitive domain*. McKay.

Bloom, B. S. (1968). Learning for mastery. *Evaluation Comment, 1*(2), 1–12. Accessed at https://files.eric.ed.gov/fulltext/ED053419.pdf on December 12, 2024.

Brodersen, R. M., & Randel, B. (2017). *Measuring student progress and teachers' assessment of student knowledge in a competency-based education system* (REL 2017–238). U.S. Department of Education, Institute of Education Sciences, National Center for Education Evaluation and Regional Assistance, Regional Educational Laboratory Central. Accessed at https://files.eric.ed.gov/fulltext/ED572995.pdf on December 12, 2024.

Burns, R. W., & Klingstedt, J. L. (1972). Introduction to competency-based education. *Educational Technology, 12*(11), 9–10.

Burriss, S. K., & Leander, K. (2024). Critical posthumanist literacy: Building theory for reading, writing, and living ethically with everyday artificial intelligence. *Reading Research Quarterly, 59*(4), 560–569. https://doi.org/10.1002/rrq.565

Buzick, H. M., Casabianca, J. M., & Gholson, M. L. (2023). Personalizing large-scale assessment in practice. *Educational Measurement: Issues and Practice, 42*(2), 5–11. https://doi.org/10.1111/emip.12551

Calabrese Barton, A., & Tan, E. (2020). Beyond equity as inclusion: A framework of "rightful presence" for guiding justice-oriented studies in teaching and learning. *Educational Researcher, 49*(6), 433–440. https://doi.org/10.3102/0013189X20927363

Camacho, D. J., & Legare, J. M. (2016). Shifting gears in the classroom—Movement toward personalized learning and competency-based education. *Journal of Competency-Based Education, 1*(4), 151–156. https://doi.org/10.1002/cbe2.1032

Carnevale, A. P., & Smith, N. (2013). Workplace basics: The skills employees need and employers want. *Human Resource Development International, 16*(5), 491–501. https://doi.org/10.1080/13678868.2013.821267

Carpenter, S. K. (2023). Optimizing learning through retrieval practice and spacing. In R. J. Tierney, F. Rizvi, & K. Ercikan (Eds.), *International Encyclopedia of Education* (4th ed., pp. 664–672). Elsevier. https://doi.org/10.1016/B978-0-12-818630-5.14078-3

Carroll, J. B. (1963). A model of school learning. *Teachers College Record, 64*(8), 723–733. https://doi.org/10.1177/016146816306400801

CASEL. (2020). *CASEL's SEL framework: What are the core competencies and where are they promoted?* Accessed at https://casel.org/casel-sel-framework-11-2020/?view=true on March 10, 2025.

Casey, K., & Sturgis, C. (2018). *Levers and logic models: A framework to guide research and design of high-quality competency-based education systems.* iNACOL. Accessed at https://aurora-institute.org/resource/levers-and-logic-models-a-framework-to-guide-research-and-design-of-high-quality-competency-based-education-systems on November 25, 2024.

Church, R. L., & Sedlak, M. W. (1976). *Education in the United States: An interpretive history.* Free Press.

Ciampa, K., Wolfe, Z. M., & Bronstein, B. (2023). ChatGPT in education: Transforming digital literacy practices. *Journal of Adolescent & Adult Literacy, 67*, 186–195. https://doi.org/10.1002/jaal.1310

Colby, R. L. (2017). *Competency-based education: A new architecture for K–12 schooling.* Harvard Education Press.

Collins, J. (2001). *Good to great: Why some companies make the leap . . . and others don't.* Harper Business.

Core Education. (2025). *Learner agency.* Accessed at https://core-ed.org/en_NZ/ten-trends/2017-ten-trends/learner-agency/ on March 26, 2025.

Costa, A. L. (2008). *The school as a home for the mind: Creating mindful curriculum, instruction, and dialogue* (2nd ed.). Corwin.

Costa, A. L., & Kallick, B. (Eds.). (2009). *Habits of mind across the curriculum: Practical and creative strategies for teachers.* ASCD.

Cotton, K., & Savard, W. G. (1982). *Mastery learning: Topic summary report—Research on school effectiveness project.* Northwest Regional Educational Laboratory. Accessed at http://files.eric.ed.gov/fulltext/ED218279.pdf on December 12, 2024.

Covey, S. R. (2020). *The 7 habits of highly effective people: Powerful lessons in personal change* (Rev. and updated ed.). Simon & Schuster.

Cuban, L. (2020). Reforming the grammar of schooling again and again. *American Journal of Education, 126*(4), 665–671. https://doi.org/10.1086/709959

Cuyacot, E. P., & Cuyacot, M. T. (2022). Competency-based education: Learner's new process for success. *International Journal of Research Studies in Education, 11*(4), 89–101. http://dx.doi.org/10.5861/ijrse.2022.165

Daniel, S., Pacheco, M., Smith, B., Burriss, S., & Hundley, M. (2023). Cultivating writerly virtues: Critical human elements of multimodal writing in the age of artificial intelligence. *Journal of Adolescent & Adult Literacy, 67*(1), 32–38. https://doi.org/10.1002/jaal.1298

Davis, D. E., DeBlaere, C., Owen, J., Hook, J. N., Rivera, D. P., Choe, E., et al. (2018). The multicultural orientation framework: A narrative review. *Psychotherapy, 55*(1), 89–100. https://doi.org/10.1037/pst0000160

DeJulio, S., Lammert, C., Hiebert, E., Avalos, A., Cagle, B., Dean, J., et al. (2024). "CATERing" to readers' needs with AI: Innovation in text design and instruction. *The Reading Teacher, 78*(1), 65–73. https://doi.org/10.1002/trtr.2345

Deye, S. (2018). *A look at competency-based education in K–12 schools*. National Council of State Legislatures. Accessed at https://web.archive.org/web/20220121015500mp_/https://www.ncsl.org/Portals/1/Documents/legisbriefs/2018/August/competencyBasedEdu_Aug2018_30_v02.pdf on December 12, 2024.

Dodson, C. W. (2019). *The critical concepts in social studies*. Marzano Resources. Accessed at www.marzanoresources.com/critical-concepts-social-studies.html on November 25, 2024.

Echols, D. G., Neely, P. W., & Dusick, D. (2018). Understanding faculty training in competency-based curriculum development. *Journal of Competency-Based Education, 3*(2), Article e01162. https://doi.org/10.1002/cbe2.1162

Education Policy Innovation Collaborative. (2021). *Competency-based education survey instrument report*. Accessed at https://epicedpolicy.org/cbe-survey-instrument-report on November 25, 2024.

Ennis, R. H. (1987). A taxonomy of critical thinking dispositions and abilities. In J. B. Baron & R. J. Sternberg (Eds.), *Teaching thinking skills: Theory and practice* (pp. 9–26). Freeman.

Ennis, R. H. (1989). Critical thinking and subject specificity: Clarification and needed research. *Educational Researcher, 18*(3), 4–10. https://doi.org/10.3102/0013189X018003004

Ennis, R. H. (2001). Goals for a critical thinking curriculum and its assessment. In A. L. Costa (Ed.), *Developing minds: A resource book for teaching thinking* (3rd ed., pp. 44–46). ASCD.

Eraut, M. (1994). *Developing professional knowledge and competence*. Falmer Press.

Evans, C. M., Graham, S. E., & Lefebvre, M. L. (2019). Exploring K–12 competency-based education implementation in the northeast states. *NASSP Bulletin, 103*(4), 300–329. https://doi.org/10.1177/0192636519877456

Evans, C. M., Landl, E., & Thompson, J. (2020). Making sense of K–12 competency-based education: A systematic literature review of implementation and outcomes research from 2000 to 2019. *Journal of Competency-Based Education, 5*(4), Article e01228. https://doi.org/10.1002/cbe2.1228

Evans, K. M., & King, J. A. (1994). Research on OBE: What we know and don't know. *Educational Leadership, 51*(6), 12–17.

Fain, P. (2014, October 27). *Big Ten and the next big thing*. Accessed at www.insidehighered.com/news/2014/10/28/competency-based-education-arrives-three-major-public-institutions on November 25, 2024.

Falicov, C. J. (2014). *Latino families in therapy* (2nd ed.). Guilford Press.

Field, K., & Feinberg, R. (2019, April 19). *Inside Maine's disastrous rollout of proficiency-based learning*. Accessed at https://hechingerreport.org/inside-maines-disastrous-roll-out-of-proficiency-based-learning on November 25, 2024.

Finn, D., & Finn, M. (2021). *Scheduling for personalized competency-based education*. Marzano Resources.

Fischer, A., Jamieson, C., Silva-Padron, G., Peisach, L., & Weyer, M. (2023). *50-state comparison: State K–3 policies*. Education Commission of the States. Accessed at www.ecs.org/50-state-comparison-state-k-3-policies-2023/ on November 25, 2024.

Fisher-Borne, M., Cain, J. M., & Martin, S. L. (2015). From mastery to accountability: Cultural humility as an alternative to cultural competence. *Social Work Education*, *34*(2), 165–181. https://doi.org/10.1080/02615479.2014.977244

Flygare, J., Hoegh, J. K., & Heflebower, T. (2022). *Planning and teaching in the standards-based classroom*. Marzano Resources.

Gagnon, L. (2023). Mastery, not time: A look at competency-based education in practice. *Childhood Education*, *99*(5), 6–13. https://doi.org/10.1080/00094056.2023.2255095

Garces, L. M., & Gordon da Cruz, C. (2017). A strategic racial equity framework. *Peabody Journal of Education*, *92*(3), 322–342. https://doi.org/10.1080/0161956X.2017.1325592

Gauthier, T. (2020). The value of microcredentials: The employer's perspective. *Journal of Competency-Based Education*, *5*(2), Article e01209. https://doi.org/10.1002/cbe2.1209

Gervais, J. (2016). The operational definition of competency-based education. *Journal of Competency-Based Education*, *1*(2), 98–106. https://doi.org/10.1002/cbe2.1011

Glossary of Education Reform. (2016). *Equity*. Accessed at www.edglossary.org/equity on November 25, 2024.

Gotto, J., Grenham, O., Kosena, B. J., Marzano, R. J., & Swanson, P. (2025). *Pioneers of personalized education: Westminster Public Schools and the pursuit of competency-based learning*. Marzano Resources.

Great Schools Partnership. (2024). *Educational equity*. Accessed at www.greatschoolspartnership.org/resources/educational-equity on November 25, 2024.

Guskey, T. R. (1994, April 4–6). *Outcome-based education and mastery learning* [Conference presentation]. Annual Meeting of the American Educational Research Association, New Orleans, LA, United States. Accessed at http://files.eric.ed.gov/fulltext/ED368770.pdf on December 12, 2024.

Guskey, T. R., & Gates, S. L. (1986). Synthesis of research on the effects of mastery learning in elementary and secondary classrooms. *Educational Leadership*, *43*(8), 73–80. Accessed at https://ascd.org/el/articles/synthesis-of-research-on-mastery-learning on December 12, 2024.

Guskey, T. R., & Pigott, T. D. (1988). Research on group-based mastery learning programs: A meta-analysis. *Journal of Educational Research*, *81*(4), 197–216. https://doi.org/10.1080/00220671.1988.10885824

Harrison, F. (2020). A common grade table inspiring meaningful feedback. *Journal of Competency-Based Education*, *5*(3), Article e01218. https://doi.org/10.1002/cbe2.1218

Hattie, J. (2009). *Visible learning: A synthesis of over 800 meta-analyses relating to achievement*. Routledge.

Hattie, J. (2012). *Visible learning for teachers: Maximizing impact on learning.* Routledge.

Hayes, H., Demeter, M., Morris, J. G., & Trajkovski, G. (2021). Transparency of cognitive complexity in performance assessments: A validity study. *Journal of Competency-Based Education, 6*(2), Article e01244. https://doi.org/10.1002/cbe2.1244

Haynes, E., Zeiser, K., Surr, W., Hauser, A., Clymer, L., Walston, J., et al. (2016). *Looking under the hood of competency-based education: The relationship between competency-based education practices and students' learning skills, behaviors, and dispositions.* Nellie Mae Education Foundation. Accessed at www.air.org/resource/looking-under-hood-competency-based-education-relationship-between-competency-based on November 25, 2024.

Haystead, M. W. (2010). *RISC vs. non-RISC schools: A comparison of student proficiencies for reading, writing, and mathematics.* Marzano Resources. Accessed at www.marzanoresources.com/risc-vs-non-risc-schools-a-comparison-of-student-proficiencies-for-reading-writing-and-mathematics.html on November 25, 2024.

Heflebower, T., Hoegh, J. K., Warrick, P. B., & Flygare, J. (2019). *A teacher's guide to standards-based learning.* Marzano Resources.

Hoegh, J. K. (2020). *A handbook for developing and using proficiency scales in the classroom.* Marzano Resources.

Hoegh, J. K., Flygare, J., Heflebower, T., & Warrick, P. B. (2023). *Assessing learning in the standards-based classroom: A practical guide for teachers.* Marzano Resources.

Hora, M. T. (2016). *Beyond the skills gap: Preparing college students for life and work.* Harvard Education Press.

Hutchison, A. (2024). Making artificial intelligence your friend, not your foe, in the literacy classroom. *The Reading Teacher, 77*(6), 899–908. https://doi.org/10.1002/trtr.2296

Iyengar, S. (2023). *Think bigger: How to innovate.* Columbia University Press.

Iyengar, S. S., & Lepper, M. R. (2000). When choice is demotivating: Can one desire too much of a good thing? *Journal of Personality and Social Psychology, 79*(6), 995–1006. https://doi.org/10.1037/0022-3514.79.6.995

Jenkins, S. (2020). *Policy solutions that foster competency-based learning.* Education Commission of the States. Accessed at www.ecs.org/policy-solutions-that-foster-competency-based-learning on November 25, 2024.

Jones, M., Avery, L., & DiMartino, J. (2020). *Putting students first: A game plan for personalizing learning.* Rowman & Littlefield.

Kelly, A. P., & Columbus, R. (2016). *Innovate and evaluate: Expanding the research base for competency-based education.* American Enterprise Institute. Accessed at https://files.eric.ed.gov/fulltext/ED566655.pdf on December 12, 2024.

Kelly, J. S. (2020). Mastering your sales pitch: Selling mastery grading to your students and yourself. *PRIMUS, 30*(8–10), 979–994. https://doi.org/10.1080/10511970.2020.1733150

Kendall, J. S., & Marzano, R. J. (2000). *Content knowledge: A compendium of standards and benchmarks for K–12 education* (3rd ed.). ASCD.

Knowles, M. (1980). Malcolm Knowles on the magic of contract learning. *Training and Development Journal, 34*(6), 76–78.

Kotter, J. P. (2012). *Leading change.* Harvard Business Review Press.

Kulik, C.-L. C., Kulik, J. A., & Bangert-Drowns, R. L. (1990a). Effectiveness of mastery learning programs: A meta-analysis. *Review of Educational Research, 60*(2), 265–299. https://doi.org/10.3102/00346543060002265

Kulik, C.-L. C., Kulik, J. A., & Bangert-Drowns, R. L. (1990b). Is there better evidence on mastery learning? A response to Slavin. *Review of Educational Research, 60*(2), 303–307. https://doi.org/10.3102/00346543060002303

Kumar, P. C., Cotter, K., & Cabrera, L. Y. (2024). Taking responsibility for meaning and mattering: An agential realist approach to generative AI and literacy. *Reading Research Quarterly, 59*(4), 570–578. https://doi.org/10.1002/rrq.570

Ladson-Billings, G. (2014). Culturally relevant pedagogy 2.0: A.k.a. the remix. *Harvard Educational Review, 84*(1), 74–84. https://doi.org/10.17763/haer.84.1.p2rj131485484751

Le, C., Wolfe, R. E., & Steinberg, A. (2014). *The past and the promise: Today's competency education movement.* Jobs for the Future. Accessed at www.jff.org/wp-content/uploads/2023/09/The-Past-The-Promise-091514.pdf on November 25, 2024.

Levine, E. (2021). *Habits of success: Helping students develop essential skills for learning, work, and life.* Aurora Institute. Accessed at https://aurora-institute.org/resource/habits-of-success-helping-students-develop-essential-skills-for-learning-work-and-life on November 25, 2024.

Levine, E., & Patrick, S. (2019). *What is competency-based education? An updated definition.* Aurora Institute. Accessed at https://aurora-institute.org/resource/what-is-competency-based-education-an-updated-definition on November 25, 2024.

Lieberman, M. (2024, September 16). It's hard to shift to competency-based learning. These strategies can help. *Education Week.* Accessed at www.edweek.org/leadership/its-hard-to-shift-to-competency-based-learning-these-strategies-can-help/2024/09 on November 25, 2024.

Lopez, S. J. (2013). *Making hope happen: Create the future you want for yourself and others.* Simon & Schuster.

Ma, W., Adesope, O. O., Nesbit, J. C., & Liu, Q. (2014). Intelligent tutoring systems and learning outcomes: A meta-analysis. *Journal of Educational Psychology, 106*(4), 901–918. https://doi.org/10.1037/a0037123

Malan, S. P. T. (2000). The "new paradigm" of outcomes-based education in perspective. *Journal of Family Ecology and Consumer Sciences, 28*, 22–28. Accessed at www.ajol.info/index.php/jfecs/article/viewFile/52788/41390 on December 12, 2024.

Manjong, N. (2023). *The impact of competency based education on educational equity* [Master's thesis, University of Central Florida]. Electronic Theses and Dissertations, 2020–2023. https://stars.library.ucf.edu/etd2020/1612

Marion, S., Worthen, M., & Evans, C. (2020). *How systems of assessments aligned with competency-based education can support equity.* Aurora Institute. Accessed at https://aurora-institute.org/resource/how-systems-of-assessments-aligned-with-competency-based-education-can-support-equity on November 25, 2024.

Marzano, R. J. (2000). *Transforming classroom grading.* ASCD.

Marzano, R. J. (2003). *What works in schools: Translating research into action.* ASCD.

Marzano, R. J. (2006). *Classroom assessment and grading that work.* ASCD.

Marzano, R. J. (2010). *Formative assessment and standards-based grading.* Marzano Resources.

Marzano, R. J. (2017). *The new art and science of teaching*. Solution Tree Press.

Marzano, R. J. (2018). *Making classroom assessments reliable and valid*. Solution Tree Press.

Marzano, R. J. (2019). *The handbook for the new art and science of teaching*. Solution Tree Press.

Marzano, R. J., & Abbott, S. D. (2022). *Teaching in a competency-based elementary school: The Marzano Academies model*. Marzano Resources.

Marzano, R. J., Aschoff, A. S., & Avila, A. (2022). *Teaching in a competency-based secondary school: The Marzano Academies model*. Marzano Resources.

Marzano, R. J., Dodson, C. W., Simms, J. A., & Wipf, J. P. (2022). *Ethical test preparation in the classroom*. Marzano Resources.

Marzano, R. J., & Hardy, P. B. (2023). *Leading a competency-based secondary school: The Marzano Academies model*. Marzano Resources.

Marzano, R. J., Heflebower, T., Hoegh, J. K., Warrick, P. B., & Grift, G. (with Hecker, L., & Wills, J.). (2016). *Collaborative teams that transform schools: The next step in PLCs*. Marzano Resources.

Marzano, R. J., & Kendall, J. S. (1996). *A comprehensive guide to designing standards-based districts, schools, and classrooms*. ASCD.

Marzano, R. J., & Kosena, B. J. (2022). *Leading a competency-based elementary school*. Marzano Resources.

Marzano, R. J., Norford, J. S., Finn, M., & Finn, D. (with Mestaz, R., & Selleck, R.). (2017). *A handbook for personalized competency-based education*. Marzano Resources.

Marzano, R. J., Norford, J. S., & Ruyle, M. (2019). *The new art and science of classroom assessment*. Solution Tree Press.

Marzano, R. J., Rains, C. L., & Warrick, P. B. (with Simms, J. A.). (2021). *Improving teacher development and evaluation: A guide for leaders, coaches, and teachers*. Marzano Resources.

Marzano, R. J., Warrick, P. B., & Acosta, M. I. (2024). *Five big ideas for leading a High Reliability School*. Marzano Resources.

Marzano, R. J., Warrick, P. B., Rains, C. L., & DuFour, R. (2018). *Leading a High Reliability School*. Solution Tree Press.

Marzano, R. J., Warrick, P. B., & Simms, J. A. (with Livingston, D., Livingston, P., Pleis, F., Heflebower, T., Hoegh, J. K., & Magaña, S.). (2014). *A handbook for High Reliability Schools: The next step in school reform*. Marzano Resources.

Marzano Resources. (2017). *Critical concepts: Scales for additional content areas*. Author.

Maslow, A. H. (1943). A theory of human motivation. *Psychological Review, 50*(4), 370–396.

Maslow, A. H. (1954). *Motivation and personality*. Harper & Row.

Maslow, A. H. (1969). The farther reaches of human nature. *Journal of Transpersonal Psychology, 1*(1), 1–9.

Maslow, A. H. (1970). *Motivation and personality* (2nd ed.). Harper & Row.

Mayfield, V. (2020). *Cultural competence now: 56 exercises to help educators understand and challenge bias, racism, and privilege*. ASCD.

McPherson, P. J. (2021). "A metamorphosis of the educator": A hermeneutic phenomenology study of the perceptions and lived experiences of the 6–12 educator in transitioning from teacher-centered to student-centered learning. *Journal of Competency-Based Education*, 6(2), Article e01230. https://doi.org/10.1002/cbe2.1230

Miller, K. (2018, June 27). Legislators vote to ease Maine's proficiency-based education mandate, allow more "local control." *Portland Press Herald*. Accessed at www.pressherald.com/2018/06/27/lawmakers-vote-to-eliminate-proficiency-based-education-mandate-in-maine on November 25, 2024.

Mitchell, D. E., & Spady, W. G. (1978). Organizational contexts for implementing outcome based education. *Educational Researcher*, 7(7), 9–17. https://doi.org/10.3102/0013189X007007009

Monahan, N. (2015, October 12). More content doesn't equal more learning. *Faculty Focus*. Accessed at www.facultyfocus.com/articles/effective-teaching-strategies/more-content-doesnt-equal-more-learning on November 25, 2024.

Morgan Consoli, M. L., & Marin, P. (2016). Teaching diversity in the graduate classroom: The instructor, the students, the classroom, or all of the above? *Journal of Diversity in Higher Education*, 9(2), 143–157. https://doi.org/10.1037/a0039716

Nagaoka, J., Farrington, C. A., Ehrlich, S. B., & Heath, R. D. (2015). *Foundations for young adult success: A developmental framework*. University of Chicago Consortium on Chicago School Research.

National Center for Education Statistics. (2024). Status dropout rates. *The condition of education 2024*. U.S. Department of Education, Institute of Education Sciences. Accessed at https://nces.ed.gov/programs/coe/indicator/coj on November 25, 2024.

National Commission on Excellence in Education. (1983). *A nation at risk: The imperative for educational reform*. U.S. Government Printing Office.

National Equity Project. (n.d.). *Educational equity: A definition*. Accessed at www.nationalequityproject.org/education-equity-definition on November 25, 2024.

National Governors Association Center for Best Practices & Council of Chief State School Officers. (2010a). *Common Core State Standards for English language arts and literacy in history/social studies, science, and technical subjects*. Authors. Accessed at https://corestandards.org/wp-content/uploads/2023/09/ELA_Standards1.pdf on November 25, 2024.

National Governors Association Center for Best Practices & Council of Chief State School Officers. (2010b). *Common Core State Standards for mathematics*. Authors. Accessed at https://corestandards.org/wp-content/uploads/2023/09/Math_Standards1.pdf on November 25, 2024.

National Research Council. (2001). *Knowing what students know: The science and design of educational assessment*. National Academies Press. Accessed at https://nap.nationalacademies.org/catalog/10019/knowing-what-students-know-the-science-and-design-of-educational on November 25, 2024.

NGSS Lead States. (2013). *Next Generation Science Standards: For states, by states*. National Academies Press.

Nodine, T. R. (2016). How did we get here? A brief history of competency-based higher education in the United States. *Journal of Competency-Based Education*, 1(1), 5–11. https://doi.org/10.1002/cbe2.1004

Noguera, P., Darling-Hammond, L., & Friedlaender, D. (2015). *Equal opportunity for deeper learning*. Jobs for the Future. Accessed at www.jff.org/idea/equal-opportunity-deeper-learning on November 25, 2024.

Núñez, A.-M. (2014). Employing multilevel intersectionality in educational research: Latino identities, contexts, and college access. *Educational Researcher, 43*(2), 85–92. https://doi.org/10.3102/0013189X14522320

Núñez, A.-M., Rivera, J., & Hallmark, T. (2020). Applying an intersectionality lens to expand equity in the geosciences. *Journal of Geoscience Education, 68*(2), 97–114. https://doi.org/10.1080/10899995.2019.1675131

OECD. (2012). *Equity and quality in education: Supporting disadvantaged students and schools*. OECD Publishing. Accessed at http://dx.doi.org/10.1787/9789264130852-en on November 25, 2024.

Oregon Department of Education. (2011). *Proficiency-based teaching and learning in Oregon: An evolution from state policy to practice*. Author. Accessed at https://digitalcollections.library.oregon.gov/nodes/view/46287 on November 25, 2024.

Pane, J. F., Steiner, E. D., Baird, M. D., & Hamilton, L. S. (2015). *Continued progress: Promising evidence on personalized learning*. RAND. Accessed at www.rand.org/pubs/research_reports/RR1365.html on November 25, 2024.

Patrick, S. (2021). Transforming learning through competency-based education. *State Education Standard, 21*(2), 23–29. Accessed at https://files.eric.ed.gov/fulltext/EJ1315095.pdf on December 17, 2024.

Patrick, S., & Sturgis, C. (2013). *Necessary for success: Building mastery of world-class skills*. iNACOL. Accessed at https://files.eric.ed.gov/fulltext/ED561282.pdf on November 25, 2024.

Patrick, S., Truong, N., & Chambers, A. (2020). *Future-focused state policy actions to transform K–12 education*. Aurora Institute. Accessed at https://aurora-institute.org/resource/future-focused-state-policy-actions-to-transform-k-12-education on November 25, 2024.

Paul, R. W. (1990). *Critical thinking: What every person needs to survive in a rapidly changing world*. Center for Critical Thinking and Moral Critique.

Porter, A., McMaken, J., Hwang, J., & Yang, R. (2011). Common core standards: The new U.S. intended curriculum. *Educational Researcher, 40*(3), 103–116. https://doi.org/10.3102/0013189X11405038

Prokes, C., Lowenthal, P. R., Snelson, C., & Rice, K. (2021). Faculty views of CBE, self-efficacy, and institutional support: An exploratory study. *Journal of Competency-Based Education, 6*(4), 233–244. https://doi.org/10.1002/cbe2.1263

Rao, T. S. S., Radhakrishnan, R., & Andrade, C. (2011). Standard operating procedures for clinical practice. *Indian Journal of Psychiatry, 53*(1), 1–3. https://doi.org/10.4103/0019-5545.75542

Reif, G., Shultz, G., & Ellis, S. (2016). *A qualitative study of student-centered learning practices in New England high schools*. Nellie Mae Education Foundation. Accessed at https://nmefoundation.org/a-qualitative-study-of-student-centered-learning-practices-in-new-england-high-schools on November 25, 2024.

Right Question Institute. (2024). *What is the QFT?* Accessed at https://rightquestion.org/what-is-the-qft on February 16, 2025.

Robinson, B., & Hollet, T. (2024). Literacy in the age of AI. *Reading Research Quarterly, 59*(4), 555–559. https://doi.org/10.1002/rrq.581

Rogers, A. P. (2021). Exploring secondary teachers' perspectives on implementing competency-based education. *Journal of Competency-Based Education, 6*(4), 222–232. https://doi.org/10.1002/cbe2.1265

Rogers, C., & Thomas, M. S. C. (2023). *Educational neuroscience: The basics.* Routledge.

Rogers, K., & Simms, J. A. (2015). *Teaching argumentation: Activities and games for the classroom.* Marzano Resources.

Ruyle, M. (with O'Neill, T. W., Iberlin, J. M., Evans, M. D., & Midles, R.). (2019). *Leading the evolution: How to make personalized competency-based education a reality.* Marzano Resources.

Ruyle, M., Awachíikaate (Cummins, J. D.), Child, L., & Dickey, D. D. (with Khalandi, H., & Weinstein, N.). (2025). *Humanized education: A mastery-based framework to promote student growth and strength.* Marzano Resources.

Ruyle, M., Child, L., & Dome, N. (with Cummins, J. D., Farragher, B., Green-Braswell, C., & Ledezma, A. V.). (2022). *The school wellness wheel: A framework addressing trauma, culture, and mastery to raise student achievement.* Marzano Resources.

Ryan, S., & Cox, J. (2017). Investigating student exposure to competency-based education. *Education Policy Analysis Archives, 25*(24). Accessed at https://files.eric.ed.gov/fulltext/EJ1137867.pdf on December 18, 2024.

Scheopner Torres, A., Brett, J., & Cox, J. (2015). *Competency-based learning: Definitions, policies, and implementation.* Regional Educational Laboratory Northeast and Islands. Accessed at https://files.eric.ed.gov/fulltext/ED558117.pdf on December 18, 2024.

Scheopner Torres, A., Brett, J., Cox, J., & Greller, S. (2018). Competency education implementation: Examining the influence of contextual forces in three New Hampshire secondary schools. *AERA Open, 4*(2), 1–13. https://doi.org/10.1177/2332858418782883

Schwartz, B. (2016). *The paradox of choice: Why more is less* (Rev. ed.). HarperCollins.

Senge, P. M. (2006). *The fifth discipline: The art and practice of the learning organization* (Rev. and updated ed.). Currency.

Sheehan, K. M. (2017). Validating automated measures of text complexity. *Educational Measurement: Issues and Practice, 36*(4), 35–43. https://doi.org/10.1111/emip.12155

Simms, J. A. (2016). *The critical concepts.* Marzano Resources. Accessed at www.marzanoresources.com/the-critical-concepts.html on November 25, 2024.

Simms, J. A. (2024). *The Marzano synthesis: A collected guide to what works in K–12 education.* Marzano Resources.

Slavin, R. E. (1987). Mastery learning reconsidered. *Review of Educational Research, 57*(2), 175–213. https://doi.org/10.3102/00346543057002175

Sommer, B., & Nchise, A. (n.d.). *Building solid evidence—It's working at Lindsay Unified.* Lindsay Unified School District. Accessed at https://docs.google.com/document/d/1cAkspEA4dkeBMh61z3w5eT-bjv2sgKADKmFm-WR1AsA/edit on November 25, 2024.

Spady, W. G. (1977). Competency based education: A bandwagon in search of a definition. *Educational Researcher, 6*(1), 9–14. https://doi.org/10.3102/0013189X006001009

Spady, W. G. (1978). The concept and implications of competency-based education. *Educational Leadership, 36*(1), 16–22. Accessed at https://ascd.org/el/articles/the-concept-and-implications-of-competency-based-education on December 18, 2024.

Spady, W. G., & Mitchell, D. E. (1977). Competency based education: Organizational issues and implications. *Educational Researcher, 6*(2), 9–15. https://doi.org/10.3102/0013189X006002009

Stanford, L. (2024, September 16). All states allow competency-based learning. Will it become a reality in schools? *Education Week.* Accessed at www.edweek.org/technology/all-states-allow-competency-based-learning-will-it-become-a-reality-in-schools/2024/09 on November 25, 2024.

Steele, J. L., Lewis, M. W., Santibañez, L., Faxon-Mills, S., Rudnick, M., Stecher, B. M., et al. (2018). *Competency-based education in three pilot programs: Examining implementation and outcomes.* RAND. Accessed at www.rand.org/pubs/research_reports/RR732.html on November 25, 2024.

Steenbergen-Hu, S., & Cooper, H. (2014). A meta-analysis of the effectiveness of intelligent tutoring systems on college students' academic learning. *Journal of Educational Psychology, 106*(2), 331–347. https://doi.org/10.1037/a0034752

Stokes, P. J. (2015). *Higher education and employability: New models for integrating study and work.* Harvard Education Press.

Surr, W., Carter, K., & Stewart, A. (2022). *Teachers making the shift to equitable, learner-centered education: Harnessing mental models, motivations, and moves.* Aurora Institute. Accessed at https://aurora-institute.org/resource/teachers-making-the-shift-to-equitable-learner-centered-education on November 25, 2024.

Sutherland, D., & Strunk, K. O. (2021). *Competency-based education in Michigan's 21j pilot districts: Case studies of implementation and innovation.* Education Policy Innovation Collaborative. Accessed at https://epicedpolicy.org/cbe-in-mis-21j-pilot-districts-case-studies-of-implementation-and-innovation on November 25, 2024.

Tetzlaff, L., Schmiedek, F., & Brod, G. (2021). Developing personalized education: A dynamic framework. *Educational Psychology Review, 33,* 863–882. https://doi.org/10.1007/s10648-020-09570-w

Thompson, D. L., & Thompson, S. (2018). Educational equity and quality in K–12 schools: Meeting the needs of all students. *Journal for the Advancement of Educational Research International, 12*(1), 34–46. Accessed at https://files.eric.ed.gov/fulltext/EJ1209450.pdf on December 18, 2024.

Toland, C. K. (2017). *Implementing proficiency-based learning: Perspectives of three Vermont high school social studies teachers* [Doctoral dissertation, University of Vermont]. ScholarWorks. Accessed at https://scholarworks.uvm.edu/graddis/673 on March 16, 2025.

Toulmin, S. E. (2003). *The uses of argument* (Updated ed.). Cambridge University Press.

Townsley, M., & Schmid, D. (2020). Alternative grading practices: An entry point for faculty in competency-based education. *Journal of Competency-Based Education, 5*(3), e01219. https://doi.org/10.1002/cbe2.1219

Tyack, D., & Cuban, L. (1995). *Tinkering toward utopia: A century of public school reform.* Harvard University Press.

Tyler, R. W. (1949). *Basic principles of curriculum and instruction.* University of Chicago Press.

Wagner, C. J. (2024). Differentiating children's reading materials with artificial intelligence: Exploring possibilities for personalized learning. *The Reading Teacher, 78*(3), 191–194. https://doi.org/10.1002/trtr.2361

Wenmoth, D. (2013). *Learner agency.* Accessed at https://web.archive.org/web/20220126110133/https://futuremakers.nz/learner-agency-2 on December 18, 2024.

Wenmoth, D., Jones, M., & DiMartino, J. (2021). *Agency by design: Making learning engaging.* Aurora Institute. Accessed at https://aurora-institute.org/resource/agency-by-design-making-learning-engaging on December 18, 2024.

World Economic Forum. (2023). *Future of jobs report 2023.* Author. Accessed at www.weforum.org/publications/the-future-of-jobs-report-2023 on December 18, 2024.

Zeiser, K., Scholz, C., & Cirks, V. (2018). *Maximizing student agency: Implementing and measuring student-centered learning practices.* American Institutes for Research. Accessed at www.air.org/sites/default/files/Maximizing-Student-Agency-NICs-Report-Oct-2018.pdf on November 25, 2024.

Zeiser, K. L., Taylor, J., Rickles, J., Garet, M. S., & Segeritz, M. (2014). *Evidence of deeper learning outcomes.* American Institutes for Research. Accessed at https://air.org/sites/default/files/2021-06/Report_3_Evidence_of_Deeper_Learning_Outcomes.pdf on November 25, 2024.

Zima, B. (2021). *Mindsets and skill sets for learning: A framework for building student agency.* Marzano Resources.

Index

A
Abbott, D. M., 79
Abbott, S. D., 48, 64, 68–69, 81, 102, 105, 111, 126, 143
academic student outcomes, 39–45
    customization and revision, 49–50
    generic proficiency scale, 42
    instructional use, 48–49
    sample proficiency scales, 42, 44
    student-friendly language, 45–47
Achieve, 3
Adams, M., 13
Adams, M., 90
Adesope, O. O., 128
advisory systems, 141–142
adult roles, 20, 22, 88, 131–133, 147
    pacing, 142–145
    professional learning, 145–146
    scheduling, 136–141
    student groupings, 133–136
    teacher-student relationships, 141–142
advocacy, 61, 78, 141–142
age-based promotion, 8
agency, 20–21, 24, 59–61
    definitions, 59–60
    environments promoting, 61–63
    reflection, 70–74
    standard operating procedures, 66–68
    student choice, 63–65
    student jobs and roles, 68–70
Ainscow, M., 80–81
alignment, 50
allow students the chance to raise previous scores, 26–27, 32–33, 107
allow students to move at a mastery pace, 27, 36–37
    sample paced-based progress report, 38
allyship, 78
alternative modes of education, 2

alternative transcripts, 36
American Association for the Advancement of Science, 3
analogical reasoning, 53
analogies, 115–116
analyzing errors in reasoning, 53
analyzing perspectives, 53
antibias attitudes, 77
anticipation guides, 112
    sample, 113
application of knowledge gained, 61
Arellanes, J. A., 79
arguments
    four elements, 122
    organization of, 123
Arrowsmith, H. E., 13
artificial intelligence, 65
Aschoff, A. S., 45, 55, 89, 99–100, 104–105, 111, 114, 124–127, 136
assessment (*see also* structure and reporting), 20, 22, 88–91
    defined, 89
    nonacademic outcomes, 96
    reliability and validity, 95
    systems, 91–94
    classroom assessment design, 94–104
    scoring and grading, 104–106
    data notebooks, 106–107
    flexibility, 19, a4–95, 104
assessments
    classroom, 92–93
    interim, 93
    nonacademic outcomes, 56–57
    obtrusive, 99–100
    student self-assessments, 102–104
    student-generated, 101
    unobtrusive, 100
    year-end, 93–94

Aurora Institute, 3
average, 104–105
Avery, L., 60
Avila, A., 45, 55, 89, 99–100, 104–105, 111, 114, 124–127, 136
Awachíikaate, 41
awareness of limitations, 80
awareness of social justice issues, 77

B

background knowledge awareness, 48
backing, 122–124
balanced assessment system, 94
Bangert-Drowns, R. L., 11
behavior, 56
behavioral regulation, 55
benchmark assessments. *See* interim assessments
Bill and Melinda Gates Foundation, 13
Bingham, A. J., 13, 90, 149–150
blended instruction, 127–128
Bloom, B. S., 2, 5, 8
Boston (Mass.) Day and Evening Academy, 3
Brett, J., 16
Brod, G., 128
Brodersen, R. M., 12
building a productive environment, 62
Bush, G. H. W., 3
Buzick, H. M., 94–95

C

Cain, J. M., 79
Calabrese Barton, A., 81–82
Camacho, D. J., 9
Carnevale, A. P., 50
Carpenter, S. K., 113
Carroll, J. B., 2, 5, 8
Carter, K., 80
Casabianca, J. M., 94–95
Casey, K., 10
celebrations, 37
Chambers, A., 37
checkpoint dates, 47
Child, L., 41
choice. *See* student choice
Chugach (Alas.) School District, 3, 6
chunking, 110–111
Cirks, V., 17
claim, 122–123
classifying, 53, 115
classroom assessment design, 94–95
    parallel assessments yield comparable scores, 97–104
    proficiency scales ensure unidimensionality and validity, 95–97
classroom assessments, 92–93
classroom learning labs, 84–85
Clinton, W. J., 3
cognitive analysis skills, 52–54, 78
    defined, 52
    knowledge application skills, 53–54
    listed, 53
cohering through standards, 5–7
collaboration
    crucial to teaching success, 110
    setting goals, 62
    setting rules, 63
    to develop standard operating procedures, 67
    skills, 21, 51, 55
collective strengths-based teaching, 136, 140–141
collective teaching approach, 140

Columbus, R., 145
Common Core State Standards (NGA & CCSSO), 3, 5
common thread, 48
CommonLit, 64
communication skills, 50–51, 55
    cross-cultural, 78
comparing, 53, 115
competence, not classification, 7–8
competency-based education (CBE), 1, 21–22
    challenges to, 25–28
    developments in the history of, 2–7
    vs. traditional education, 7–11
    practices, 11–20
competency-based grouping, 125–126
competency-based pacing, 142–145
competency-based practices, 11
    implementation challenges, 149–150
    decision making as a link between vision and system, 18–20
    proven effects on student learning, 11–12
    various possibilities, 12–18
complex tasks, 110, 117–121
    associated steps, 118–120
complex thinking skills, 50
components of CBE and CBE-adjacent approaches, 13–17
Comprehensive Guide to Designing Standards-Based Districts, Schools, and Classrooms (Marzano & Kendall), 3
conflict resolution, 78
considerations for assessment
    nonacademic outcomes, 56–57
Consoli, M. L. M., 82
constructing support, 53
content-area bullpens, 138
content-area saturation, 136, 139–140
    sample, 140
contextual behavior, 51
continuum of competency-based scheduling approaches, 136
Cooper, H., 128
Core Education, 60
Council of Chief State School Officers, 3, 5
Cox, J., 16
creating analogies, 115–116
creating metaphors, 115–116
creativity, 51
critical thinking skills, 51
cross-cultural communication, 78
Cuban, L., 21, 25
cultural awareness and competency, 77–83
    year-end assessment inequity, 93–94
cultural humility, 79–80
cultural responsiveness, 19
Cummins, J. D., 41
cumulative review, 124
customization and revision of proficiency scales, 49–50
Cuyacot, E. P., 142
Cuyacot, M. T., 142

D

daily data collection, 81
Darling-Hammond, L., 76
data notebooks, 106–107
Davis, D. E., 79
decision making, 118
    skills, 52–53
    vital link between vision and system, 18–20
declarative knowledge, 114–116
Demeter, M., 40

demonstration classroom, 83
developmental approach, 80
developments in the history of CBE, 2–4
    expanding education and promoting mastery, 4–5
    cohering through standards, 5–7
Dewey, J., 2, 4
Deye, S., 13
dialogue, 78
Dickey, D. D., 41
DiMartino, J., 10, 17, 60
Dodson, C. W., 101
Dusick, D., 145

E

Echols, D. G., 145
Education Policy Innovation Collaboration, 36, 60
Educational Technology, 2
efficacy, 59
Ehrlich, S. B., 60
Ellis, S., 16, 142
empathy, 77
engaging in complex tasks, 127
environment promoting agency, 61–62
    questions for creating a partnership learning model, 62
equity, 19–22, 24, 75–78
    definitions, 75–76
    inequitable teacher quality, 83–85
    power dynamics, 78–81
    systemic injustice, 81–83
Ethical Test Preparation in the Classroom (Marzano et al.), 101
Evans, C. M., 11, 14–15, 76–77, 89–90, 94, 110, 142–143, 149–150
examining similarities and differences, 127
examples of fact and opinion, 122
examples of mastery, 47
expansion of public education in the U.S., 2, 4–5
experiential power, 79
experimental inquiry, 53, 119
explicit learning outcomes, 19

F

Fain, P., 131
Falicov, C. J., 82
Farrington, C. A., 60
feedback loops, 62
Finn, D. III, 34
Finn, M., 34
Fischer, A., 9
Fisher-Borne, M., 79
flexibility, 110
    in assessment practices, 119
    in grouping, 125–126
focus, 54
focused instruction time (FIT), 136–138
    as part of a lunch rotation, 137
    collective strengths-based teaching, 140–141
    content-area saturation, 139–140
    organization around competencies, 138–139
formative scores, 104
format-specific scores, 98–99
foundational knowledge, 8–9
foundational skills, 50
four elements of an argument, 122
Friedlaender, D., 76
function frames, 101
Future of Jobs Report (World Economic Forum), 6

G

Gagnon, L., 8, 151
Garces, L. M., 78
Gates, S. L., 11
Gauther, T., 51
generate-sort-connect, 112
generating and defending claims, 110, 121–124
    examples of fact and opinion, 122
    four elements of an argument, 122
    organization of an effective argument, 123
generating mental images, 47, 53
generating/pursuing one's own standards for performance, 54
Gervais, J., 14
Gholson, M. L., 94–95
Glossary of Education Reform, 75
goal setting and reflection, 61
Goals 2000: Educate America Act, 3
Gordon da Cruz, C., 78
grading. *See* scoring and grading
graduate profiles, 39
Graham, S. E., 76–77
the grammar of schooling, 21
graphic organizers, 124
Great Schools Partnership, 76
Grift, G., 110
grounds, 122–123
grouping students (*see also* instructional groups and centers), 133–136
    by age, 134–135
    by proficiency, 133–134
    communication is critical, 135
growth mindset, 55
    development, 60
    reminders, 57
guaranteed and viable curriculum, 19
    defined, 39–40
Guskey, T. R., 11

H

habits of success, 51
Hardy, P. B., 28, 35, 39–40, 83, 128, 138, 146
Harrison, F., 10, 105
Hattie, J., 102
Hayes, H., 40–41
Haynes, E., 12–14, 30
Haystead, M. W., 11
Heath, R. D., 60
Heflebower, T., 110
Hendricks, M., 79
High Reliability Schools framework, 18
Hoegh, J. K., 110
Hwang, J., 6

I

implementation challenges, 149–150
iNACOL, 3
inclusive practices (*see also* equity), 21–22
    language, 77
independence, 62
inequitable teacher quality, 83–85
initiative, 21
instruction, 20, 22, 109, 128–129
    blended, 127–128
    instructional groups and centers, 125–127
    instructional unit design, 110–125
    mastery-oriented, 19
instructional coaching, 145–146
instructional groups and centers, 125–127

instructional rounds, 84
instructional unit design, 110–111
    chunking, 110–111
    generating and defending claims, 110, 121–124
    previewing, 110–113
    processing and practicing, 110, 114–117
    recording and representing, 110, 113–114
    reviewing and revising, 110, 124–125
    undertaking projects and complex tasks, 110, 117–121
instructional use of proficiency scales, 48–49
    teacher uses, 49
interim assessments, 93
intersubjective power, 79
invention, 53, 119
investigation, 53, 120

J

Jamieson, C., 9
Jenkins, S., 14–15, 39
Jones, M., 10, 17, 60

K

Keller, F., 2
Kelly, A. P., 145
Kelly, J. S., 15
Kendall, J. S., 3
knowledge application skills, 52–54
    defined, 53
    listed, 53–54
knowledge maps, 115–116
Kosena, B. J., 10, 40–41, 51, 53, 59, 83–84, 92–93, 106, 110, 133–134, 136, 138, 140
Kulik, C.-L. C., 11
Kulik, J. A., 11

L

Ladson-Billings, G., 93
Landl, E., 11, 14
Le, C., 4, 6
leadership skills, 50
learning action plans, 106–107
"Learning for Mastery" (Bloom), 2
learning gaps, 8–9
learning materials, 80
learning progressions, 28
learning targets, 57, 107
    descriptions of, 106
    well-defined, 61, 91
learning walks, 85
Lefebvre, M. L., 76–77
Legare, J. M., 9
Lehigh (Mich.) Public Schools, 84–85
Levine, E., 7, 15, 41, 128, 142
Lieberman, M., 1
lifelong learning, 80
Lindsay (Calif.) United School District, 12
linear trend, 105
Liu, Q., 128
Lopez, S. L., 59
Lowenthal, P. R., 16, 131

M

Ma, W., 128
Malan, S. P. T., 15
Manjong, N., 8
Marin, P., 82
Marion, S., 15, 89–90, 94

Martin, S. L., 79
Marzano Resources, 45
Marzano, R. J., 3, 10, 25, 28, 30, 34–35, 39–41, 43, 45, 47–48, 51–53, 55–56, 59, 65, 66–69, 81, 83–84, 89, 92–94, 96–106, 110–111, 114, 117, 120, 124–127, 132, 136, 133–138, 140, 143, 146
Maslow, A. H., 121
Maslow's hierarchy of needs, 121
Mastery Learning Movement, 2
mastery-based metrics, 24
mastery-oriented instruction, 19
Mayfield, V., 19
McMaken, J., 6
McPherson, P. J., 110, 132, 145, 149
measurement topics, 28
memory, 113–114
mentorship, 80
Mercier, C., 79
metacognition, 51
    defined, 54
metacognitive skills, 54–55, 78
    listed, 54–55
metaphors, 115–116
minority students
    year-end assessment inequity, 93–94
Monahan, N., 131
Morris, J. G., 40
motivation and engagement, 51, 61

N

Nagaoka, J., 60
A Nation at Risk (NCEE), 2, 5
National Center for Education Statistics, 9
National Commission on Excellence in Education, 2, 5
National Council on Education Standards and Testing, 3
National Education Standards and Improvement Council, 3
National Educational Goals Panel, 3
National Equity Project, 76
National Governors Association (NGA), 3
National Research Council, 3, 94
National Science Teachers Association, 3
Nchise, A., 12
Neely, P. W., 145
Nesbit, J. C., 128
The New Art and Science of Teaching model (Marzano), 110
Next Generation Science Standards (NGSS Lead States), 3, 5
Nodine, T. R., 8
Noguera, P., 76
nonacademic student outcomes, 39–40, 50–52
    cognitive skills, 52–54
    considerations for assessment, 56–57
    metacognitive skills, 54–55
    personal relational competencies taught in Westminster (Colo.) Public Schools, 52
    self-care skills, 55–56
Norford, J. S., 34
Núñes, A.-M., 78
NWEA Measures of Academic Progress, 93

O

OECD, 76
omnibus grade, 28, 30
ongoing assessment, 11
opportunities to raise previous scores, 26–27, 32–33
    sample measurement topics, 33

opportunity to learn, 2
organization around competencies, 136, 138–139
    sample, 139
organization of an effective argument, 123
organizational power, 78
outcomes-based education, 2

P

pacing, 142–145
    by mastery, 9–10
    sample, 144
parallel assessments
    defined, 97
    obtrusive assessments, 99–199
    student self-assessments, 102–104
    student-generated assessments, 101
    translation of all scores into a common scoring scheme, 98
    unobtrusive assessments, 100
    yield comparable scores, 97–99
"parking lot," 81
participation, 56
part-to-whole discussion, 48
Patrick, S., 7, 15–16, 37, 128, 142
"peaks and valleys," 81
peer feedback, 47
Peisach, L., 9
Pelc, N., 79
personal initiative, 62
personal relational competencies, 51
personal tracking matrix, 102–104
    sample, 103
Personalized System of Instruction (Keller), 2
perspective taking, 77
Pigott, T. D., 11
Porter, A., 6
portrait of a graduate, 39
poverty, 41
    inequitable teacher quality, 83–85
    year-end assessment inequity, 93–94
power dynamics, 78–81
    types of power, 78–79
power-law trend, 105
practices, 1
    competency-based, 11–20
practicing new knowledge, 126
predictability, 41
previewing, 110–113
    anticipation guide for ratios and percentages, 113
problem-solving skills, 50–51, 53, 118–119
procedural domains, 21–22
    adult roles, 88, 131–147
    assessment, 88–107
    instruction, 88, 109–129
procedural knowledge, 117
processing and practicing, 110, 114
    declarative knowledge, 114–116
    knowledge maps, 115–116
    procedural knowledge, 117
processing new knowledge, 126
professional learning communities, 110
professional learning, 145–146
proficiency levels, 19, 28, 41–45, 78, 87–88
    generic proficiency scale, 42
    sample proficiency scales, 42, 44
    student-friendly language, 45–47
proficiency scales
    customization and revision, 49–50
    defined, 41
    ensure unidimensionality and validity, 95–97
    facilitate content chunking, 111
    generic, 42
    instructional use, 48–49
    keeping students engaged with, 48
    mistake educators make when constructing, 43–44
    samples, 42, 44
    teacher uses, 49
    vs. rubrics, 42
project-based learning, 117–121
    seven-step process, 120–121
Prokes, C., 16, 131
promoting mastery, 4–5
prompts, 70–71
    promoting reflection, 72–74
proven effects of CBE practices on student learning, 11–12
pushing the limits, 54

Q

qualifiers, 122–124
Question Formulation Technique (Right Question Institute), 71–74
questions
    for creating a partnership learning model, 62
    for planning centers, 127
    promoting agency, 72–74
    prompting, 70–71
    to develop agency, 67–68
    to give students choice, 65
    to guide decision making about adult roles, 133–134
    to guide decision making on assessment, 90
    to guide instruction and planning, 109
    to prompt reflection, 72–74

R

Randel, B., 12
rational and organized thought processes, 51
readiness, 150–151
ReadWorks, 64
real-world applications, 47
recording and representing, 110, 113–114
reflection, 21, 61, 107
    before, during, and after learning, 71
    defined, 70
    important element of agency, 70–74
    prompts, 47
Reif, G., 16, 142
Reinventing Schools Coalition, 3, 11–12
relationship skills, 52
relevance, 150–151
reliability of assessment, 95
    series of scores over time provide, 97
representational power, 79
require mastery of all outcomes, 26–27, 35
require mastery of some outcomes, 26–27, 34–35
resisting impulsivity, 55
resources, 150–151
responsibility to others, 64
responsibility to self, 64
responsibility to the environment we share, 64
retakes. See allow students the chance to raise previous scores
reviewing and revising, 110, 124–125
rewards, 47
Rice, K., 16, 131
Right Question Institute, 71
rightful presence, 82

Rogers, A. P., 16
Rogers, C., 113
Rogers, K., 121–122
roles. *See* student jobs and roles
routines, 41
rubrics vs. proficiency scales, 42
Ruyle, M., 41, 75
Ryan, S., 16

S

safety, 41
salient identities, 80
scheduling, 136–137
    collective strengths-based teaching, 136, 140–141
    content-area saturation, 136, 139–140
    continuum of competency-based scheduling approaches, 136
    focused instruction time, 136–138
    organization around competencies, 136, 138–139
Scheopner Torres, A., 16
Schmid, D., 17
Schmiedek, F., 128
Scholz, C., 17
Schults, G., 16, 142
scoring and grading, 104–106
    accuracy, 10
seeking accuracy, 54
seeking clarity, 54
seeking cohesion and coherence, 55
seeking incremental steps, 54
self-actualization, 121
self-administered preassessment, 48
self-assessment, 107
    students, 10
    teachers, 84
self-awareness, 52
self-care skills, 55–56
    self-system skills, 56
self-efficacy, 24, 51
self-reflection, 79
self-regulation, 21, 52, 55
    agency, 60
self-system skills, 56, 78
setting goals and making plans, 55
seven-step process for projects, 120–121
Sheehan, K. M., 95
Silva-Padron, G., 9
Simms, J. A., 101, 121–122
Smarter Balanced Assessment Consortium, 12
Smith, N., 50
Snelson, C., 16, 131
social awareness, 52
social promotion. *See* age-based promotion
Sommer, B., 12
Spady, W. G., 25
standard operating procedures, 66–68
    defined, 66
Standards Movement, 3
standards
    cohering through, 5–7
    development of, 3–4
state assessments. *See* year-end assessments
state tests. *See* year-end assessments
Steenbergen-Hu, S., 128
Steinberg, A., 4
Steward, A., 80
Steward, R. L., 13, 90

structural domains, 21–22, 23–24
    agency, 24, 59–74
    equity, 24, 75–85
    structure and reporting, 24–38
    student outcomes, 24, 39–57
structure and reporting, 20–21, 24–28, 37–38
    allow students the chance to raise previous scores, 26, 32–33
    allow students to move at a mastery pace, 26, 36–37
    implications for grading, 27
    require mastery of all outcomes, 26, 35
    require mastery of some outcomes, 26, 34–35
    teach and report outcomes, 26, 30–31
    teach outcomes but report overall grade, 26, 28–29
Strunk, K. O., 16–17, 60, 63, 84–85, 116–117, 146
student choice, 21, 63–65
    suggestions for balancing freedom and support, 64
student groupings, 133–136
student jobs and roles, 62, 68–70
student outcomes, 20–21, 39–41
    academic, 41–50
    nonacademic, 50–57
student roles. *See* student jobs and roles
student self-assessments, 102–104
    personal tracking matrix, 103
student voice, 21, 61
student-friendly language, 45–47
    instructional use, 48–49
    student-friendly versions of a proficiency scale, 46–47
student-generated assessments, 101
student-led conferences, 62
Sturgis, C., 11, 16
suggestions for balancing freedom and support, 64
summative scores, 104
Surr, W., 80, 150
Sutherland, D., 16–17, 60, 63, 84–85, 116–117, 146
systemic injustice, 81–83
systems analysis, 53, 120
systems of assessment, 91–94
    comprehensive competency-based, 92

T

Tan, E., 81–82
task management, 61
teach and report outcomes, 26–27, 30–31
    sample report card for individual outcomes, 31
teach outcomes but report overall grade, 26–27, 28–30
    sample scoring, 29
teacher quality. *See* inequitable teacher quality
teacher's role, 131–132
teacher-student relationships, 141–142
teamwork, 50, 55–56
test anxiety, 100
Tetzlaff, L., 128
Thomas, M. S. C., 113
Thompson, D. L., 76, 83
Thompson, J., 11, 14
Thompson, S., 76, 83
three Rs of school-level change, 150
Toland, C. T., 132
Townsley, M., 17
toxic stress, 41
traditional education
    competence, not classification, 7–8
    difficulty around changes, 25–28

foundational knowledge, 8–9
grading accuracy, 10
ongoing assessment, 11
pacing by mastery, 9–10
vs. CBE, 7
Trajkovski, G., 40
transcendence, 121
transparency, 41, 57
   defined, 40
trauma, 41
triggering wonder, 61
Truong, N., 37
Tyack, D., 21, 25
Tyler, R. W., 2, 4–6

U

undertaking projects and complex tasks, 110, 117–121, 127
   complex tasks and associated steps, 118–120
unidimensionality, 95–97
   defined, 95

V

validity of assessment, 95–97
   defined, 96
various possibilities, 12–18
   components of CBE and CBE-adjacent approaches, 13–17

visualizing, 47, 53, 111–112
vocabulary lists, 106–107

W

Warrick, P., 110
Washburne, C., 2, 4
weekly conferences, 81
Wenmoth, D., 10, 17, 41, 61–64, 68
Westminster (Colo.) Public Schools, 7, 12, 18–20, 26, 34, 37, 47, 50–52, 85, 99, 134, 142
Weyer, M., 9
What Is Competency–Based Education? (Levine & Patrick), 7
Winnetka Plan, 2, 4
Wipf, J. P., 101
Wolfe, R. E., 4
work completion, 55–56
working in groups. *See* teamwork
World Economic Forum, 6
Worthen, M., 15, 89–90

Y

Yang, R., 6
year-end assessments, 93–94

Z

Zeiser, K. L., 17
Zima, B., 60–61, 70

Marzano Academies Series

The Marzano Academies series presents a blueprint for success with competency-based education from experts and educators who have done this work. Leaders and teachers at the elementary and secondary levels will gain innovative, equitable, and effective practices for schools and classrooms.

BKL056, BKL055, BKL053, BKL054

Assessing Learning in the Standards-Based Classroom
Jeff Flygare, Tammy Heflebower, Jan K. Hoegh, and Philip B. Warrick

Whether you are well versed in writing proficiency scales or are seeking practical guidance on classroom assessment that best supports student learning, this book will help you design standards-based assessments that provide meaningful data to inform your next steps in the instructional cycle.

BKL070

Mindsets and Skill Sets for Learning
Bill Zima

Rely on *Mindsets and Skill Sets for Learning* to help you cultivate confident thinkers who have a strong sense of agency over their lives. Use this guide to enhance your classroom culture with targeted, student-centered learning.

BKL051

The New Art and Science of Classroom Assessment
Robert J. Marzano, Jennifer S. Norford, and Mike Ruyle

Design assessment for learning and drive student engagement and academic achievement. Gain holistic assessment methods and tools for both summative and formative assessment in the classroom, and transition to a mode of assessment that truly reflects course curriculum and student progress.

BKF788

Visit MarzanoResources.com or call 888.849.0851 to order.

MARZANO Resources

The Marzano Compendium
Your go-to source for research-based solutions

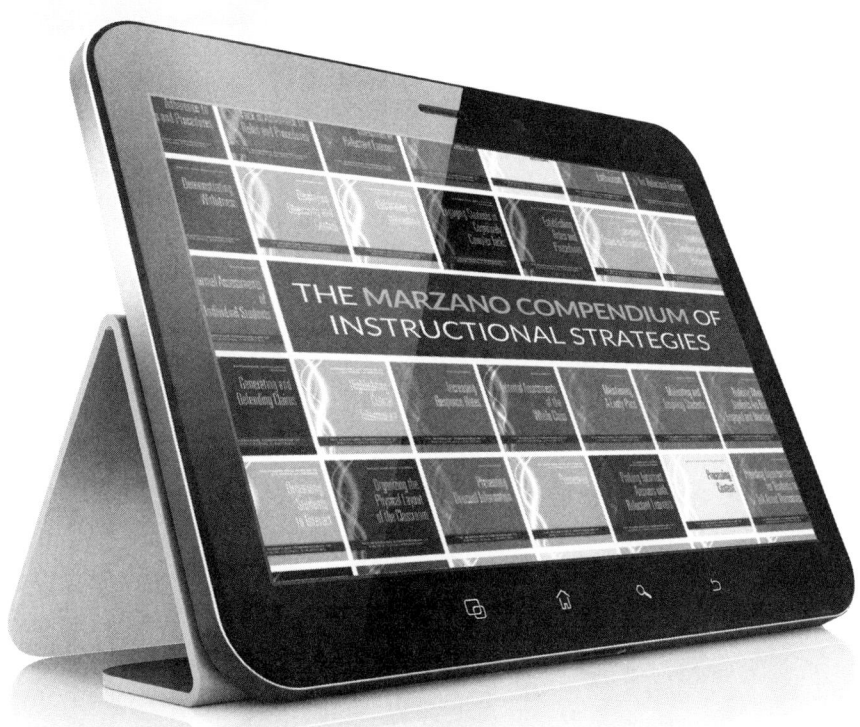

Developed for teachers, instructional coaches, teacher mentors, and administrators, this easy-to-navigate online resource combines and updates content from Dr. Marzano's most popular titles, including *The New Art and Science of Teaching*, *Becoming a Reflective Teacher*, and *Coaching Classroom Instruction*.

Gain access to:
- 43 folios, explaining each element in depth
- More than 300 research-based instructional strategies
- Resources for students and teachers
- Surveys to track progress
- Videos explaining the elements and categories of The New Art and Science of Teaching framework
- 24x7 online access

Learn more
MarzanoResources.com/Compendium